The self-destruction of lives and reputations among the rich and famous of our society has reached epidemic proportions. One after the other, great men *.e falling like dominoes as they defy the profound wisdom of scripture, make :hemselves into their own god and satisfy their most base desires. If you are already experiencing substantial fame, power or wealth or, more importantly, if you are approaching that possibility in your life, this will be one of the most important books you will ever read.

– **Barry Meguiar,** *President/CEO of Meguiar's, Inc, and host of FOX's Speed Channel program* Car Crazy Television

This book is a jolting reminder of how small (but bad) decisions in a leader's life can end in disaster for himself and others. A must, must read for all pastors, church and parachurch leaders; executives of companies and denominations; as well as others. Dr. Goodall writes with passion, conviction and compassion for those that have had great failures and about what we can learn from these examples. For some this book can be a marriage, ministry and life saved. *WHY GREAT MEN FALL* is also about how great men need not fall.

– **Don Wilkerson**, *Executive Director, Global Teen Challenge*

Wayde Goodall has shared a brief but masterful guide to leadership in *WHY GREAT MEN FALL.* Having known Wayde as an exceptional leader for over 20 years, it is obvious that this is the life story and lessons learned by a great, humble leader whose "life lessons" blended with the truth of God's Word give us a page turner that addresses the personal issues of today. Secular and sacred leaders would do well to read this work and adhere to the principles Wayde outlines so well to avoid the pitfalls of leadership and, yes, to accomplish lasting legacies.

– **Dr. Tom Phillips,** *Director of the Billy Graham Cove & Director of Crusades for Billy Graham Crusades*

The Bible encourages us to "take heed lest you fall." Wayde Goodall has provided us with critical insight into why great men fall. But more than that, he offers a positive roadmap to finish well and avoid becoming another statistic.

– **E. Glenn Wagner,** *President, FutureLead, Former Vice President of Promise Keepers*

Anyone can read the headlines. It takes a finer mind to go behind the faces of scandalized celebrities and their lurid exploits. Dr. Goodall combines discernment, insight, and an engaging contemporaneity to turn the tale of the fallen into wisdom for those willing to learn.

– **Mark Rutland,** *President, Southeastern University*

Why Great Men Fall

Wayde Goodall

First printing: May 2005
Second printing: February 2006

ISBN-13: 978-0-89221-622-2
ISBN-10: 0-89221-622-0
Library of Congress Control Number: 2005925563

Cover by Left Coast Design, Portland, Oregon

Printed in the United States of America

Please visit our website for other great titles:
www.newleafpress.net

For information regarding author interviews,
please contact the publicity department at (870) 438-5288.

New Leaf Press
A Division of New Leaf Publishing Group

Acknowledgment

I want to thank my wife and best friend Rosalyn (who is a college instructor in technical and professional writing) for her patience, advice, reading, and editing. Also, she once said to me that I was her "lifelong project." She has greatly encouraged me to stay on balance and keep focused on the right thing.

CONTENTS

PREFACE

For over three decades I have had the privilege of working with leaders. Watching talented people succeed because of hard work, great ideas, and wise choices is a thrill. Watching them go too far, risk too much, and make choices that compromise their career and family is shocking and very sad. A thousand times I have thought:

> *Why did he decide to have that affair?*
> *What thought process did he go through to persuade himself to take that ethical risk?*
> *The price he paid for what he did was everything.*

What causes (especially) men to risk it all?

We have seen leader after leader make bad decisions that caused the bottom to fall out of their lives. Everyone can make bad decisions . . . whether it is the president, the CEO, the priest, or a well-known athlete, it hits the front page of *USA Today*. Almost daily we read about another CEO, CFO, university president, politician, athlete, or minister who has done something that basically ruined their lives.

Over the years, I have observed at least 14 different characteristics that seem to be the tipping points for these leaders in their decisions to do wrong. All of us have these basic tendencies, however, some develop them to a point where they go over the edge. I will point out the patterns to help us understand why the decisions were made.

This is more than just a book that reveals the problem or points a finger at the guilty. You will learn solutions, guidelines, and boundaries that we can put around our lives that will protect us from our intentional wrong choices. Also, we will explore the notion of hope, if you have made a decision that could affect your life in the wrong way. All of us have made mistakes, bad calls, been selfish, and didn't think through our actions as thoroughly as we should have.

But we do not have to make a habit of bad behavior, and there is a way out of the slippery slope of doing the wrong thing.

Throughout history, great men have made wrong decisions that have radically changed their lives. However, there are some who have made bad choices, and decided to learn from it, grow through it, and become even a greater leader.

> Though he fall, he shall not be utterly cast down;
> *For the Lord upholds him with His hand*
> (Psalm 37:24; NKJV).

1

WHY GREAT MEN FALL

LET HIM WHO THINKS HE STANDS
TAKE HEED LEST HE FALL

(1 COR. 10:12; NASB).

What do you think of when you hear the following names:

Kobe Bryant (NBA player)
Jimmy Swaggart (television evangelist)
Gary Condit (congressman)
Bill Clinton and Monica Lewinsky

You may also have heard of:

Andrew Fastow, Ken Lay, and Jeff Skilling (ex-CFO and CEOs of Enron)
Ben Glisan (Enron's "whiz kid," now serving five years in prison)
Dennis Kozlowski (former Tyco International chief executive)
Mark Swartz (Tyco's ex-CFO)
Bernie Ebbers (CEO of WorldCom)
Scott Sullivan (WorldCom ex-CFO)
Paul Patton (Kentucky Governor)
Sampson and Delilah
David and Bathsheba

What do you think of when you hear the occupation of "Catholic priest"? My thoughts, and I'm sure the thoughts of millions of others, are:

- How in the world could these people let themselves do this?
- Why did they give up so much for so little?
- They worked hard for what they had — why did they give it up for that?
- What would make them compromise their dreams?

In reality we are asking, "What was the cause of this great man's fall?"

Many who ask "why" fear that the same thing could happen to them. They should be concerned . . . because it could. All of us are vulnerable. We have feet of clay and successful people have fallen since the beginning of mankind. Adam did. Cain did. Abraham lied; his son Isaac did the same. At all levels, among all genders, ages, cultures, occupations, and positions, people have made decisions that cost them too much.

Some ask "why" because they fear for their organization, university, company, or church. When a leader falls, it is expensive. It can take months, years, and possibly decades to rebuild confidence and trust. Productivity and fruitfulness are lost.

Others ask "why" with a cynical "I told you so." They don't trust leadership — never have — and likely never will. They have been hurt, set up, disappointed, and have watched or experienced this kind of thing before. Their attitude is:

> All leaders are basically manipulators — that's how they got there.

> Leaders don't care about us little guys and if they do — they do it for their own benefit.

> That professional athlete (or CEO) can buy his success.

Debby Then, L.A. psychologist and author, said, "Every week, you see somebody in your friendship circle or at work or in the popular media who has committed adultery. This topic just never goes away."[1] Adultery, lying, "moving the numbers," manipulation, and under-the-table decisions can be part of any office or family.

In researching her book, *Not Just Friends*, Shirley Glass found that 25 percent of wives and 44 percent of husbands have had extramarital intercourse.[2] Many of their affairs began at work. She found that from 1982 to 1990, 38 percent of unfaithful wives in her clinical practice were involved with someone from work. From 1991 to 2000, the number of women's work affairs increased to 50 percent. Men also are having most of their affairs with people from their workplace. Among the 350 couples she has treated, approximately 62 percent of unfaithful men met their affair partners at work.[3] Seeing the same people for legitimate reasons frequently helps friendship develop.

There are reasons people make bad choices, and it doesn't happen overnight. There is an evolution — one thought, decision, or move at a time. They decided to go to the wrong place, ask the wrong question, look at illegal or immoral materials, or have a conversation with someone they knew was compromising. The behavior began somewhere. When their lives are analyzed, there are hints, oversights, and road bumps. The thought process had been going on, but the decision wasn't made until the opportunity presented itself.

I don't believe this kind of "life altering" failure just hits like a brick on some particular day. There is a process — sometimes it can be short lived — sometimes it works on a person for years. Some call it temptation, others call it a hazard of success.

Some men who have begun walking on the precipice of compromise call it a perk of their position and believe that they have rights that others do not have. Their thoughts may be, *I've earned this and I deserve it because of who I am.*

Some actually have the ability to do something morally wrong, and then walk into another room and conduct business in a professional way. For instance, a minister that I once talked with met ladies in the bar of whatever hotel he was staying in (the hotel that was near the church he was speaking in on Sunday). He would lie about his career, get her to his room, and do his thing. Then, somehow, he would isolate that behavior in a "mental room" and go to sleep, wake up in the morning, and preach about righteousness. That doesn't make sense to most of us, but some have become really good at compartmentalization.

Others expect their peers and subordinates to keep quiet about what they see or hear. Executives, CEOs, CFOs, politicians, pastors, priests, etc. can all begin to rationalize. I believe that people with tremendous responsibility and powerful influence within their company or community should be well compensated, but how much is too much? What behavior crosses the line? There is a line. How far is too far?

Regardless of how long it took before they were caught or why they thought they could do it — the end result was the same. Incredible loss — shock to those who admire them — distrust in the organization — hundreds leave the church. Many of us put the newspaper down and ask ourselves, 'Are there any leaders out there that we can trust?"

There are and you can be one of them.

You know it and I know it. Life is full of hazards — temptations and situations where we can compromise. People will challenge us, question us, and try to subtly and not so subtly get us off track. Some have watched our mentor, leader, or even father or mother get to their position by "bending the rules" or getting away with . . . (you fill in the blank).

As we aim for our target and walk down the road (or the fast-moving highway) to reach our goals, we can spot the hazards. If we look hard and think about it, we can see the "mines" just below the surface of this minefield called life. We will recognize when we are operating under the radar of what is safe, right, true, and legal.

If we avoid life's hazards, we will save ourselves an incredible amount of money, relationships, trust, and time. Many successful men have walked away from compromise. There are plenty of examples of leaders who made tough decisions and held their moral ground.

Ethical and moral compromise certainly does not have to be part of the process or the perks of becoming a leader. You *can* win, lead, direct, set goals, and do the right thing.

The mines in this battlefield are words, concepts, truths, and patterns.

There are at least 14 possibilities for failure. Yours might look a little different from mine. The thought might come to you in the middle of a meeting or you could begin thinking that "he is getting away with it, so should I." Great men fall for a variety of reasons. Ask yourself these questions as you build a protective fence around your life:

- Do I feel a sense of entitlement? — "I deserve this because of who I am or what I do."

- Am I a gifted entrepreneur — but my life is out of balance?

- Do I have the ability to compartmentalize my moral choices? Can I do something wrong and then mentally put it aside while I do something right?

- Do I expect my employees and peers to keep quiet when I do questionable things?

- Am I a "high risk" man who loves the adrenaline rush of danger or compromise?

- Am I a magnet for women? Do they love my power, money, influence, and personality?

- Is my integrity in check?

- Am I surrounded with "yes men" with very little accountability?

- Do I compromise my conscience?

- Who is my mentor? Who am I a mentor to?

- Do I play by my own rules? Do I have an ethical code?

- Do I handle stress in a healthy way?

- What do I do with my money? Integrity includes both my physical and my financial self.

- Are my moods under control?

- Have I found a balance with money, sex, and power?

The following chapters will speak to all of these issues as we remember that men who are stronger than you and me have made very bad decisions. Men who are weaker — have made good decisions. The gift of choice can be the greatest blessing you have and it can be the *choice* that can severely damage you. Sometimes we avoid failure, but other times our action costs us everything.

But remember that *the temptations that come into your life are no different from what others experience.* And God is faithful. He will keep the temptation from being so strong that you can't stand up against it. *When you are tempted, he will show you a way out* so that you will not give in to it (1 Cor. 10:13;NLT, emphasis added).

Endnotes

1. "She Stayed with a President Who Strayed," *USA Today* (June 10, 2003): p. 8D.

2. Shirley Glass, *Not Just Friends* (New York, NY: The Free Press, 2003), p. 3.

3. Ibid., p. 2.

2

ENTITLEMENT (I DESERVE THIS . . .)

EVEN THE SON OF MAN DID NOT
COME TO BE SERVED, BUT TO
SERVE, AND TO GIVE HIS LIFE A
RANSOM FOR MANY
(MARK 10:45; NASB).

For centuries, theologians and philosophers have tried to explain why a religious king, who had everything he could want, would have a "one night stand" with his neighbor's wife.

King David had it made. He was winning all the battles, had amassed great wealth, had a strong family, but wanted someone who belonged to someone else: ". . . when she came to him, he lay with her . . ." (2 Sam. 11:4).

It could have been lust; possibly a weak moment. Or the real possibility of thinking, *I'm the king, I can do anything I want, and I've earned the right. I am entitled to this.*

The answer to why is found in the following chapter.

The Lord sent Nathan to David. And he came to him, and said, "There were two men in one city, the one rich and the other poor. The rich man had a great many flocks and herds. But the poor man had nothing except one little ewe lamb which he bought and nourished; and it grew up together with him and his children. It would eat of his bread and drink of his cup and lie in his bosom, and was like a daughter to him. Now a traveler came to the rich man, and he was unwilling to take from his own flock or his own herd, to prepare for the wayfarer who had come to him; rather he took the poor man's ewe lamb and prepared it for the man who had come to him" (2 Sam. 12:1–4; NASB).

Although the rich man had everything and the poor man had only one thing, the rich man thought that because of "who he was" he could take the only thing the poor man had. This illustrates what King David did.

The sense of entitlement goes beyond getting your deserved and agreed-upon income, perks, and benefit package. It can get out of control when you begin thinking:

> *I'm the boss; where would they be without me?*
>
> *I've worked hard for this company; they need to take good care of me. I'll do whatever I feel like doing.*
>
> *I'm the anointed one, the pastor, apostle, prophet, bishop, and I can do this because of who I am.*

This was where King David was. He took from someone else, took advantage of a person who really couldn't say no, to satisfy his desire.

In our country, on CNN, FOX, all the networks, and in a huge spread in *USA Today* was the story, "Kentucky Governor Paul Patton tearfully acknowledged an affair and announced that he would not run for the U.S. Senate." Later, respected *Chicago Tribune* columnist Bob Greene resigned in October after acknowledging that he had a sexual relationship with a girl in her late teens.[1] Congressman Gary Condit was alleged to have had an affair with Chandra Levy. President Clinton acknowledged a sexual liaison with a young intern in the Oval Office. Yes — in the White House. Sounds crazy, but it happens all the time with powerful men.

Baltimore psychologist Shirley Glass said, "For certain prominent men, (it) goes along with their position. It is part of the culture they live in." Author Peggy Vaughan said, "These men have a different mindset . . . there is a sense among the very powerful that they work very hard and deserve whatever they want. They are 'go-ahead' guys accustomed to getting whatever they want. They don't ask themselves why. They ask, 'Why not?' "[2]

It's an all-too-common story of a once wonderful leader (maybe a company or church's founder) who had great ideas, goals, and strategies for his organization. After he leaves his position, he puts a guilt trip on the next leader or board that they still owe him "something" . . . indefinitely. Instead of walking away with his head held high and saying, "I did my best for the years I served and was adequately compensated," he says, "I was the best. I made this thing what it is. They need to recognize that and compensate me for as much as I decide, and for as long as I want them to." What got into this guy? Possibly ego, anger, resentment, whatever; his attitude convinced him that the company or church was continually indebted to him.

Marital therapist Michele Weiner-Davis says of some leaders, "They believe they are above it all. They won't be found out. They can outsmart the system."[3]

Most don't go so far as to engage in adultery, financial fraud, or tax evasion. Some begin with decisions to eat at the finest restaurants and stay in the best hotel rooms, have room service, etc., when it is at their organization's expense. Some start with excessive use of the company credit card, or with working fewer hours, or by not being accountable to anyone. In their opinion, they always have a right. They ignore their wife's warnings when she tells them, "It's all going to your head," or "You're beginning to believe your own press releases." If the company can (and wants to) pay for a perk and it's in the open, that's one thing, but if the company can't afford it and doesn't really want to give you something, and you take it anyway, then it's another thing. Leaders are compensated differently, and that's not the issue. Leaders work hard, put in long hours, and make huge decisions that benefit their organizations. Their position is critical — their leadership often greatly helps their company and perhaps even saves it because of their knowledge and influence. But, if leaders are not careful to walk the line of integrity and practice good ethics — things can easily get out of control. Where do rights, perks, and service expectations turn from okay and balanced to not okay and out of balance? Authors David Dotlich and Peter Cairo write, "If Othello were CEO of Enron and Oedipus Rex in charge of WorldCom, they might well have made the same mistakes as Jeff Skilling and Bernie Ebbers. In tragedies both ancient and modern, leaders fall because of arrogance. Defined as 'excessive pride' and an inflated view of self-worth, arrogance routinely derails the best and the brightest. It thrives on success, confidence, and ego, and if you have plenty of any of these, beware! Many current and former CEOs, such as Gary Wendt, Martha Stewart, Durk Jager, and Robert Horton, have been described as arrogant, and that perception contributed to their failure in the top jobs."[4]

Where's the integrity in the extreme decision to take what you want because of who you perceive you are? What throws a great leader off? On what

ENTITLEMENT (I DESERVE THIS . . .)

day did he decide that he could write his own rules? It's gradual, it's subtle, and it has destroyed many brilliant leaders.

On the other hand, many leaders, perhaps most, had the same temptations but kept their lives in balance. Jim Copeland, who retired from Delotte Touche Tohmatsu as CEO, remained squeaky clean during the time Arthur Anderson, Enron, and numerous corporate scandals within accounting firms were breaking the rules. He often returns to Georgia and Norcross First Baptist Church, where he was once chairman of the deacons and taught Sunday school for 25 years. The church provides visitor parking spaces close to the front door, but he won't use them, choosing instead to park with the members. He prays when he wakes up every morning. In an interview, sitting next to his wife, he volunteered that he has never "run around" on her and can't understand how anyone who is unfaithful can be ethical in business.[5] Was Jim Copeland paid well? Yes. Did he have excellent benefits in his job? Yes. Did he have a corporate jet? No. Jim drew a line in the sand and said, "I'll not go any further."

♣ ARROGANCE IS WHEN YOU THINK YOU'RE RIGHT, AND EVERYONE ELSE IS WRONG.

Another story — Al Dunlap, formerly CEO of Sunbeam, made radical decisions after he became CEO. He was applauded for reducing labor costs, closing factories, and controlling expenses. He was nicknamed "Chainsaw Al," because of his incredible disregard for the impact his decisions had on the workers. "What is less well known is that while undertaking these actions, Dunlap gave himself large pay increases, first-class air fares, and a free Mercedes. Although the Sunbeam headquarters was in Florida, Dunlap demanded the right to stay at the Four Seasons Hotel when he visited his dentist in Pennsylvania, among other executive perquisites he required to help him manage the demands and stress of the job.

"Dunlap's style has since been discredited, and he endured and settled shareholder lawsuits about his role as CEO. But his case is illustrative and not entirely different from that of many leaders who come to identify with their appointed role, believing in not only their infallibility but also their entitlement."[6] The sense of entitlement can cover a lot of territory. It could be in the area of adultery, the excessive use of corporate credit cards, or the opinion that he never has to say, "I'm sorry," because he is never wrong. There are written rules in every successful company and church, and there are unwritten ethical codes that every leader must follow.

In case you think this happens only to people in power — think again. It could be an employee who thinks the boss really *needs* him because of his abilities, so the employee expects unusual perks and treatment. This employee says to himself, "That boss needs to realize that it will be very hard to replace me," or, "Without me, this company wouldn't make it." It might be a board member in the church who thinks he can push the pastor around because of his influence in the congregation. It might be people who attend a church who think they're entitled to have the pastor serve their whims. No matter what time of day it is or what the pastor or priest might be doing, they feel they are entitled to extra, on-the-spot, personal care.

Kids can do this to their parents; parents can do it to their children. Employees can do it to their boss; bosses can do it to their employees. Pastors can do this to their congregation and congregation members can do it to their pastors. Operating "under the radar" of what is right can affect us all.

My phone rang and on the other end was a desperate pastor. To make a long story short, he had regularly been using cocaine right before he preached on Sunday mornings because he thought he needed an "energy boost" to help him communicate effectively and energetically to his congregation. What was going on? First, he thought that whatever the cocaine did for him was the emotional and physical demonstration that his congregation wanted. He thought that without it he could not communicate effectively. And he thought he could get away with it. He had gotten away with it so far, but, he had become dependant and addicted and wanted to quit — and couldn't.

Somehow he thought, *The people need to see me perform because this is what they really want in their pastor.* He then rationalized that because of their need, he was entitled to some extra help. He would just get a little high on drugs and become what they wanted him to be. He felt entitled to this illegal activity.

A sense of entitlement can have a devastating impact on your organization, your family, or your church. It subtly slips into your life — first one rationalization, then another. There are many leaders who know they demand too much and that they expect to have the best of everything. What they don't recognize is that they are ruining their future. Others see what they are doing and the necessary foundation of trust is eroded. The most common negatives of the sense of entitlement are:

- Getting stuck in our own world view. We stop growing, we stop learning, and we no longer need the team. Every leader must be a life-long learner. A leader is a reader and the team is critical to the success of the company. To be successful, we must surround ourselves with great thinkers and doers.

ENTITLEMENT (I DESERVE THIS . . .)

- Feeling that we don't need to answer to anyone — boards, committees, staff, or our wife. We have told ourselves that we don't need accountability. If mistakes are made, we blame everyone except ourselves.

- Being unwilling to change. We think that our way is the only "really right" way. We don't listen to the opinions of other wise, well-educated, or experienced people. If someone disagrees with us — we write them off.

- Thinking we are infallible. We believe we do everything with excellence and — in the world of executives — we are really the best. This blindness can slowly invade our lives. We may have a great education, have many years of experience, have risen to a level in the organization where we call the shots, but do not see that infallibility is an illusion. We cause a lot of problems when we feel we make the right call every time. All of us have weaknesses. There are people in our companies who have more education, experience, and "horse sense" in many areas. We need them because all of us are fallible.

Entitlement is an illness that can be self-medicated. It's not a trap that we inevitably walk into. All leaders can watch out for this temptation, by looking within.

Examine your life and see if you're claiming to be entitled to something that is not yours. Before "entitlement" ruins you, prevents you from achieving success, or destroys your church or company — you can choose to get it under control. As you climb the ladder of success you often get more perks; people admire and flatter you. You got there because you believed in the vision. You worked hard, walked through open doors, and one thing happened after another. But now you surround yourself with "yes" people. Anyone who challenges your opinion is your enemy. You feel you deserve more money, perks, time, service, agreement, and empowerment because of who you are. What do you think? Is it excessive? Are you in balance? If there's excess, you can choose to get your life into balance. Educate yourself by looking at others who have abused their situations — and have failed. It's not worth the price they paid.

When you look at others who have crossed the integrity line, ask yourself, "Was it worth it?" I have talked to many men who have committed adultery. One day they decided to talk with, to touch, or to have sex with someone who wasn't their wife. Many of these men left their wife, children, home, friends, and church because they thought they could not control their "testosterone high." I've seen pastors lose their family and church and even walk away from their God. I've watched leaders lose their money, their children, their respect, their integrity, and their peace. Was it worth it?

Explore your world and see if there are people who love you but will still tell you the truth. Do you understand that because of who you are people might not tell you the truth? Your position alone can intimidate those who work for you — or if you're a pastor or priest — those who sit in the pew. Do you have anyone within your organization who is loyal to the company and you, but will tell you where the "yellow flags" are? Is there anyone in your life who will point out excesses, wrong attitudes, and arrogance? Remember Nathan — King David's counselor? He did that for David.

Excessive pride will make us unaware of the small failures that are symptoms of the big failure that could destroy us.

In every company, family, church, and government there are small failures. No one is perfect — except God. Does your pride keep you from recognizing the small failures? If we don't, these little issues will prevent us from being effective. If we think, *They don't realize who I am — I'm the proven leader,* we will miss the little things that can eventually turn into the major thing that will ruin our organization or us.

"High risk executives grow used to special consideration in everything they do . . . they see themselves as entitled to get their needs met," says Janis Abrahms Spring, author of *How Can I Forgive You.*[7] Failure can be our friend. It can teach us what not to do. It can be a warning of an even greater failure. Pride doesn't allow us to pay attention. Pride believes, "I deserve all of this." "Pride goes before destruction, and a haughty spirit before a fall" (Prov. 16:18; NKJV).

This chapter began with the tragic story of how King David felt entitled. David wasn't always that way. Over the years, after victories, parades, and praise, he slowly became that way. When David started out, he was running for his life. God had chosen him to be the leader, but he had many enemies. He was hungry, eager, and humble, and he listened to people's advice. One day, David was trapped in a cave with the enemy all around. He was thirsty, the Bible tells us, " 'Oh, that someone would get me a drink of water from the well near the gate of Bethlehem!' So the three mighty men broke through the Philistine lines, drew water from the well near the gate of Bethlehem and carried it back to David. But he refused to drink it; instead, he poured it out before the LORD. 'Far be it from me, O LORD, to do this!' he said. 'It is not the blood of men who went at the risk of their lives?' " (2 Sam. 23:15-17; NIV).

David's men felt he was entitled to a drink of water. He probably was. But David decided not to demonstrate any sense of entitlement because other people had risked their lives for his desire.

ENTITLEMENT (I DESERVE THIS . . .)

Evidence of entitlement can cause people's stories to hit the front pages of newspapers or it can be so subtle that it is known only to their family and friends. Either way — it can lead to the downfall of wonderful leaders and organizations.

Endnotes

1. "Add to the List of Affairs to Remember," *USA Today* (October 2, 2002): p. 12D.

2. Ibid., P. 12D.

3. Ibid., p. 12D.

4. David L. Dotlich and Peter C. Cairo, *Why CEOs Fail* (San Francisco, CA: Jossey-Bass, 2003), p. 2.

5. "Retiring Deloitte CEO Built His Career on Integrity," *USA Today* (May 30, 2003): p. 9B.

6. Dotlich and Cairo, *Why CEOs Fail*, p. 11.

7. Jane O'Donnell and Greg Farrell, "Business Scandals Prompt Look into Personal Lives," *USA Today* (November 5, 2004): p. 2B.

3

Entrepreneurs without Balance

The Assumer of Risk

The world thrives on "risk takers." New businesses, challenges, start-ups, people's dreams, and visions are all part of what drives industry, and it is what we are impressed with. We need visionaries — people who dream a bigger dream and courageous leaders who are willing to take a chance.

The word "entrepreneur" is often defined as a person who is willing to take the risk of not making a profit and who gets a profit when there is one.[1] Millions of entrepreneurs begin their day early and work late, create jobs, and are good corporate citizens. They're what America is known for.

Leaders of change see change as an opportunity. They thrive on it. Entrepreneurial leaders take on risk as a necessary attribute of being a leader. Peter Drucker said, "A change leader looks for change, knows how to find the right changes, and knows how to make them effective both outside the organization and inside it. To make the future is highly risky. It is less risky, however, than not to try to make it."[2]

But . . . when one's being entrepreneurial is out of balance — it is dangerous. Many powerful men love the danger of risk and thrive on it. Like a NASCAR driver, the heart beats faster; the pressure is what they thrive on, and the race is the passion of their life. The adrenaline rush of being over the edge and walking in areas where few have walked is addictive. This "high" keeps them going and makes them feel successful, creative, and on top of their game. The need to push harder can grow with age. When it's not thought out, evaluated, and the risk is haphazardly entered into — failure can be the result. And we have watched many entrepreneurs fall in recent years.

The founders of companies and religious organizations are largely the ones who have committed the corporate scandals that continuously hit the front pages of the paper. These entrepreneurial CEOs had the initial vision to create and then crossed over to bend the rules of the law. "When you're the founder, you think you can do anything and that the rules don't apply to you," says Mark Cheffers, CEO of AccountingMalpractice.com. That "can lead to behavior that is inappropriate," says Joseph Carcello, professor of accounting at the University of Tennessee. Carcello reported that the founder or original CEO was the top executive at the time of the misconduct in 45 percent of the 303 fraud cases studied between 1987 and 1997.[4]

Risk, courage, faith, and boldness are necessary to lead. However, there is a dark side to this. Since the beginning of time, countless people with tremendous ability have decided to go too far and lose most or all they had acquired. Some common temptation factors run in the veins of the entrepreneurial leader.

The Sense that Enough — Isn't Enough

The Bible tells us, "King Solomon was greater in riches and wisdom than all the other kings of the earth. The whole world sought audience with Solomon to hear the wisdom God had put in his heart" (1 Kings 10:23–24; NIV).

Solomon was the "Bill Gates" of the world and more. Not only was he rich, smart, and gifted, he was a world leader that other leaders envied. Kings and leaders wanted just to listen to him, walk around his country, observe how he led, and see what he owned. People of his time knew that this king was unique, dynamic, and had talents that they wanted to try to attain. The rule of "success leaves clues" was just as true then as it is today and anyone who watched Solomon was looking for the clues.

There is no question that he was an entrepreneurial leader. He started all kinds of programs that developed his nation, and, as a result, became the wealthiest man on earth. Though Solomon had more than anyone could imagine at the time, he wanted more. He understood the rules. His father was a great leader, too, and was careful to explain to Solomon the principles and directives to live by. He also had the history of laws that were passed down to him through the generations. However, somehow he decided not to obey them. One decision, one day, and one person at a time — he began writing his own rules.

His downfall? "King Solomon, however, loved many foreign women. . . . They were from nations about which the LORD had told the Israelites, 'You must not intermarry with them, because they will surely turn your hearts after their gods.' Nevertheless, Solomon held fast to them in love. . . . As Solomon grew old, his wives turned his heart after other gods" (1 Kings 11:1–4; NIV). The story could be in today's newspaper. "He loved women." "He wanted more." "He led a secret life."

Solomon, the lead entrepreneur of his day, lost much of what he had. His nation became divided, his wisdom became confused, his clear vision became foggy, and his solid opinion of right and wrong ended up encouraging immorality, cruelty, and dishonoring God. He wanted more so badly — that he decided to do the wrong thing.

The desire for more is often so strong that it pushes many over the edge. Ken Lay, the CEO of Enron for 15 years, sold 1.8 million shares of Enron stock. What's wrong with selling stock? The problem is that while he was CEO the majority of the company's alleged fraud occurred — conflict of interest, padding his accounts, or whatever you call it. His sale equaled $101 million. His multimillion-dollar salary and perks weren't enough.

Adelphis, WorldCom, Enron, Homestore, Waste Management, and HealthSouth all had bad accounting that was lead by their entrepreneurial founders when their alleged misconduct occurred.

"The desire to get rich is a remarkable motivator behind many of the USA's great innovators. But the temptation can get perverted thanks to gratuitous stock options and bonuses . . . they have every incentive to get richer," says Jack Ciesielski, president of R.G. Associates.[5]

When is enough — enough?

ENTREPRENEURS WITHOUT BALANCE

They Believe That "What I Do — Is Me"

Someone said, "Ask a woman who she is and she will tell you how she feels. Ask a man who he is and he will tell you what he does or what he owns." Entrepreneurial leaders often put so much time, energy, and life into the business that *they become the business*. It is their life. Their life is what they do. They lose their sense of personal identity.

The definition of the company, church, or organization is the definition of who they are. Sometimes, as a result, the finances become their personal "piggy bank." They think they deserve it and are entitled to anything they want. After all, without their leadership where would the company, church, or organization be?

Somehow, the courage that it took to start the organization becomes personal ownership. The pastor who can't give up the church he started to the next leader so that it can thrive again feels that no one can do it quite like him. The CEO that hangs on too long feels that giving up his position means giving up his life. The founder of the company can't walk away because he doesn't really have any other life outside of his work.

It becomes illegal when the leader feels the company's (or church's) resources are his personal property. The confusion? What I do for a living is really me. "I do it, therefore I have a right to own it. I started it; I was the brains behind this organization, so I have the right. . . ."

Many leaders that have fallen because of this deception really believe that they were entitled to everything they took. Why? The organization was their "baby" and they gave birth to it.

They Begin Believing Their Press Releases

Great leaders have great exposure. The press, the community, and people who are watching them say wonderful things about them. The words, accolades, and hungry eyes of the admiring crowd feel great, even though deep inside most know that the comments are not well founded. Success is a highly sought-after experience, and when a "winner" is evident it catches the eye of the crowd.

Entrepreneurs often become heroes to their followers. As a result, a lot of followers become "yes men." Who is going to say no to the leader? Who will say, "I think we are going too far, we are out of balance, or we are breaking the rules"?

> In their blind conceit, they cannot see how wicked they really are (Ps. 36:2; NLT).

If the CEO goes down — most of the time the CFO goes down. Why? Were they involved in the misconduct from the beginning? Probably not. Most of the time the CFO saw something — many things — and decided to turn his head. They too became calloused when fudging the books, or bending the law. They didn't want to challenge the one who made the company. Sometimes the CEO made the CFO's silence, worthwhile — either financially or career wise. As a result, when the CEO went down — so did the CFO.

YOU CAN BE AN ENTREPRENEURIAL RISK TAKER WHO DOESN'T FALL

The dangers of the entrepreneur who is out of balance are all around us. Risk is not a bad thing. Not thinking, not seeking advice, or trying to write your own rules when taking risk can be. We must always have people who are willing to change things for the better, dream the new dream, and go after ideas that no one has tried. Being aware of the mistakes and publicized failures that others have made can warn us and insulate us from doing the same thing.

I believe that everyone has an entrepreneurial tendency; some are driven by this energy, and some are afraid to venture into new areas in life. The desire to create comes from the One who created us.

Some guidelines for those who want to create:

The Gift of Imagination . . . Entrepreneurial People Are Visionaries

Peter Drucker said, "I once attended a university symposium on entrepreneurship at which a number of psychologists spoke. Although their papers disagreed on everything else, they all talked about an 'entrepreneurial personality,' which was characterized by a 'propensity for risk taking.' A well-known and successful innovator and entrepreneur who had built a process-based innovation into a substantial worldwide business in the space of twenty-five years was then asked to comment. He said: 'I find myself baffled by your papers. I think I know as many successful innovators and entrepreneurs as anyone, beginning with myself. I have never come across an "entrepreneurial personality." The successful ones I know all have, however, one thing — and only one thing — in common: they are not "risk takers." They try to define

> ♣ THEY ARE NOT "RISK FOCUSED"; THEY ARE "OPPORTUNITY FOCUSED."
> PETER DRUCKER[6]

the risks they have to take and to minimize them as much as possible. Otherwise, none of us could have succeeded.' "[7]

Vision, seeing the big picture, dreaming the dream, and calculated risk are all involved in the entrepreneurial personality. The Bible tells us "Where there is no vision, the people perish" (Prov. 29:18; KJV).

Vision is the ability to see what something — or someone — can become. Truth is involved in a great idea. Doing the right thing is involved when one is leading in the vision casting and development. Not compromising right communication, but being committed to consistently obeying the rules is also part of entrepreneurial leadership.

When one sees the big picture of what an organization could become he sees opportunity. Reaching the "opportunity" involves doing the right thing one day at a time.

Thinking Before Doing

All leaders have to take risks. However, that doesn't mean that they are not to think. I believe that a definition of faith is "calculated risk." Risk isn't reckless.

Part of being an entrepreneurial leader means that you dream the dream, see the goal, and calculate the cost. Jesus said, "Suppose one of you wants to build a tower. Will he not first sit down and estimate the cost to see if he has enough money to complete it? For if he lays the foundation and is not able to finish it, everyone who sees it will ridicule him, saying, 'This man began to build and was not able to finish' " (Luke 14:30; NIV).

> ❧ YOU AND YOUR
> ORGANIZATION
> NEED TO KEEP
> GROWING.
> — PETER DRUCKER[8]

Starting without calculation is foolish. Taking the promotion without thinking about the cost is dangerous. The risk involved in reaching the goal is commendable; however, taking the risk without thinking about what it will cost you, your family, and others is not good.

John Maxwell said, look at wise leaders who take risks, and you find that they:

- Gather information wisely
- Risk from strength
- Prepare thoroughly
- Fail successfully

- Display flexibility
- Observe timing
- Envision what can be gained
- Understand what is at stake
- Stay on mission
- Possess the right motives
- Give their followers wins
- March forward with confidence[9]

Frederick Smith, CEO of FedEx Corporation, said that entrepreneurs understand the "process of self-education. They find out what's necessary to run bigger enterprises through a lot of different educational and resource channels. Second, they surround themselves with people on the board, or within management who have a lot of experience. For example, Michael Dell, who's a good customer of ours, brought in some professional managers to help him make the transition. So I think there's a pretty clear path how you get there. The difficulty comes in the personal discipline that's required to do it."[10]

Peter Drucker says, "Everyone in a pharmaceutical company knows that the company's survival depends on its ability to replace three-quarters of its products with entirely new ones every ten years. But how many people in an insurance company realize that the company's growth — perhaps even its survival — depends on the development of new forms of insurance? The less spectacular or prominent technological change is in a business, the greater the danger that the whole organization will ossify, and more important, therefore, is the emphasis on innovation."[12]

> ❧ YOU ALWAYS HAVE TO BE AN ENTREPRENEUR, OTHERWISE YOU WILL FALL BEHIND.
>
> — FRED SMITH (FEDERAL EXPRESS)[11]

Taking the time to think, evaluate, and getting wise advice are necessary ingredients for successful leadership. Jumping to conclusions, taking risks without thinking, and ignoring the "yellow lights" of life is arrogant and dangerous. Too many great leaders made of the same stuff as us have decided to do their own thing and not listen to good information. Many haven't taken the time to think it through and, as a result, were given time to think about what they have done.

ENTREPRENEURS WITHOUT BALANCE

When you are thinking about the risk of change, there are some questions that can be asked:

- Will this decision or promotion help me with my spiritual life, family, and personally, or will it take from these priorities in my life?
- What is motivating me to do this? Authority, money, security, helping people?
- How will this decision change what I do, how I live my life, and how will it affect those I care about?

Being Brave

Leadership is lonely. The entrepreneur that fell made the decision to compromise alone. He can't blame it on anyone else. At the same time, the leader who decides to do the right thing decided to do this alone. Martin Luther King Jr. said, "The time is always right to do what is right."[14]

Being courageous is in the blood of the entrepreneurial leader. They are informed risk takers; they often see what no one else sees, and they have the courage to take action on it.

> ☙ COURAGE IS CONTAGIOUS. WHEN A BRAVE MAN TAKES A STAND, THE SPINES OF OTHERS ARE OFTEN STIFFENED.
> — BILLY GRAHAM[13]

When I was in the navy I was involved in the Vietnam war. My home was the USS *Fox*, which is a guided missile destroyer. As we patrolled the Tonkin Gulf and performed our duty of protecting the aircraft carrier, I often walked the decks in the humid tropical nights and watched the flashes of light when a bomb would explode. I frequently thought, *I wonder who died?* or, *Who is the brave man that is leading that command tonight?* I felt that the men and women on shore — in the jungle — were fighting a different war than me, one that took more courage.

One of those men was a leader named Colonel H. Norman Schwarzkopf. He commanded the First Battalion of the Sixth Infantry. His responsibility was the Batangan Peninsula. This location was fought over for decades and was full of mines, hidden tools of destruction, and booby traps that took many of our young men's limbs and lives.

Schwarzkopf felt that part of his responsibility was to not only find ways to cut down on the casualties, but whenever a man stepped on a mine he would personally fly out and evacuate the man on his helicopter.

On one occasion a man walked into the middle of a minefield. Not realizing the ground was full of mines, this young soldier stepped on the hidden bomb and it severely injured his leg. He began screaming, tried to crawl away, and cried out for help.

As Colonel Schwarzkopf watched, he immediately thought that he could help him. In his autobiography, *It Doesn't Take a Hero,* he wrote, "I started through the minefield, one slow step at a time, staring at the ground, looking for telltale bumps or little prongs sticking up from the dirt. My knees were shaking so hard that each time I took a step, I had to grab my leg and steady it with both hands before I could take another. . . . It seemed like a thousand years before I reached the kid."[15]

> ❧ IT IS NOT FAIR TO ASK OF OTHERS WHAT YOU ARE NOT WILLING TO DO YOURSELF.
> — ELEANOR ROOSEVELT

The young officer who wrestled while attending West Point knew how to hold him down. He pinned him to the dirt, talked to him, and saved his life. The courage from within changed a young man's life.

Without the courage to take calculated risks and take the steps to accomplish the dream, new inventions, prescriptions, companies, safeguards, "homeland security," and helpful technology would not happen.

The Bible tells us about a time when there was no "frequent vision" (1 Sam. 3:1; ESV). This was a time when there were no leaders with courageous integrity. The dream of getting better, becoming stronger as a nation, reaching new goals of helping people and changing lives for good was forgotten for many decades.

No one saw the big picture, and at that time there was no one who was brave enough to do something about the desperate situation that their nation was in.

Many of our organizations and churches have lost their vision — their dream. As a result, they are stagnant or dying. Every leader knows that conflict is often involved in change; however, every organization must change. The courageous leader understands the transition of implementing change and does it.

The Bible tells us that there was a man who was willing to listen and do something about the desperate situation in his nation. "Then the Lord called Samuel, and he said, 'Here I am!' " (1 Sam. 3:4; ESV).

ENTREPRENEURS WITHOUT BALANCE

"Then the Lord said to Samuel, 'Behold, I am about to do a good thing . . .' " (1 Sam. 3:11; ESV).

Samuel was the entrepreneurial leader of his day. He was willing to change things for the better. He wanted to hear about what needed to be done to improve the situation — and revive the nation.

"Here I am!" Within this statement there is incredible courage. Samuel was saying, "I want to see the big picture and I want to be the one to see the 'vision' that has been missing." He was also saying, "When I see the vision, I will be willing to take the courageous risk that will be involved in implementing it."

As a result, "As Samuel grew, and the Lord was with him and let none of his words fall to the ground . . . and all of Israel . . . knew Samuel was established . . ." (1 Sam. 3:19–20; ESV).

Entrepreneurial leaders are visionaries and have the gift of imagination.

Entrepreneurial leaders think before they act.

Entrepreneurial leaders have the courage to change the way things are.

Endnotes

1. *World Book Dictionary* (Chicago, IL: Thorndike/Barnhart, 1988), p. 707.
2. Peter E. Drucker, *The Daily Drucker* (New York: Harper Business, 2004), p. 69.
3. Ibid.
4. Matt Krantz, "Experts Say CEOs Entrepreneur Traits May Lead to Trouble," *USA Today* (May 12, 2003): p. B.01.
5. Ibid.
6. Ibid.
7. Drucker, *The Daily Drucker*, p. 74.
8. Ibid., p. 77.
9. John C. Maxwell, *The Right to Lead* (Nashville, TN: Countryman, 2001), p. 66.
10. Thomas J. Neff and James M. Citrin, *Lessons from The Top* (New York: Doubleday, 1999), p. 279.
11. Drucker, *The Daily Drucker*, p. 74.
12. Ibid., p. 77.
13. Maxwell, *The Right to Lead*, p. 23
14. Ibid., p., 23
15. Ibid., p. 14.

4 COMPARTMENTALIZATION

"ANYONE . . . WHO KNOWS THE
GOOD HE OUGHT TO DO AND
DOESN'T DO IT, SINS."

JAMES 4:17; NIV

EMOTIONAL, BEHAVIORAL ROOMS

We've all wondered how a particular person can do the things they do and seemingly not feel bad about it.

A cry for help from Bob on the telephone told me that he wanted out of his hideous pornography addiction. Bob is a leader in his community and was involved in something that was destroying his life. He said, "Wayde, you're the last person I'm calling. If you can't help me, I believe my marriage is over. I know that it's only a matter of time until my wife and my company finds out what I'm doing. I'm out of control."

"What's going on Bob?" I asked.

"I started looking at a few off-color (pornographic) pictures on my computer — I was just curious. It became more than curiosity when I started thinking about when I'd be able to do it again."

"Bob does your wife know? Where do you do this — at home, the office?"

"No, I don't dare tell her. She'd freak out. I do it at home when she thinks I'm doing office stuff and I'm doing it at work when my door's closed."

"How did you get to this point?" I asked.

"At first, I didn't feel bad — no big deal." He explained, "I justified it, thought it was just fantasy; I wasn't doing things with real people. I was able to do it and not let it bother me. Now, I can't get it out of my mind."

Bob's dilemma was that he still had a conscience. Being bothered by his wrong behavior was healthy.

A sensitive conscience is good. Compartmentalizing isn't necessarily bad. Remaining sensitive and keeping our focus is a discipline.

Compartmentalization is an ability that we as leaders must have. The challenge is to keep our focus while all kinds of mental noise is going on. As leaders, we need to be able to have a difficult discussion with an employee who needs correction, then, in the next minute, walk into the boardroom and have all of our emotions in check. Besides helping me exercise, compartmentalization helps me do what I do for a living. I try to exercise and run six days a week. Normally I run a daily 5K, but once a week I try to do a 10K. I'm ok at it — and some who know me tell me I would probably place or win for my age category in a race. Now — don't challenge me to a race, because, like most men, I'm competitive. I'll die trying to beat you! My biggest challenge in running isn't pain, breathing, knees, ankles, hips, or getting up in the morning; it's trying not to think about what I'm doing. When I think about my running — while I'm running — I think about how *far* I've run, how *long* I've been running, and how far I need to go. When I think about something else and just put my legs in "drive," the time and miles fly by. Compartmentalization is learned. While it's our friend when we need to concentrate on the "now," it can be our enemy when we use it to ignore wrong behavior. We can put different aspects of our lives into different mental rooms — emotional drawers. We can even get to the point where we do things that we once realized were wrong and think we are not "really" harming anyone.

In one mental room, we are committed to our marriage and family and what we do for a living, but in another mental room, we do things that could ruin our marriage, family, and career. Concerning those who have adulterous encounters, Peggy Vaughan, in her book *The Monogamy Myth*, says, "They are able to ignore, rationalize, and not consider the consequences."[1]

The Bible says it is dangerous to walk on the edge of wrong behavior. "Can a man scoop fire into his lap without his clothes being burned?" (Prov. 6:27; NIV). Our conscience tells us where the line is. Many walk closer and closer to the line, and rationalize their behavior until severe damage is done.

Psychologist Shirley Glass tells us, "Good people in good marriages are having affairs. Well-intended people who never intended to be unfaithful are unwittingly forming deep, passionate connections before they realize they've crossed the line that separates platonic friendship from romantic love. Today's workplace and the Internet have become the new danger zones of attraction and opportunity — the most fertile breeding grounds for affairs. In the new crisis of infidelity, more and more marriages are being threatened by friendships that have slowly and insidiously turned into love affairs."[2]

Cybersex is one of the most popular activities of compartmentalization. "The computer is a tantalizing 21st century sex toy that looks benign but can explode like a land mine, trashing the private and work lives of a surprisingly large number of Americans," says psychologist Kimberly Young. "Contrary to popular belief, cybersex addiction isn't a problem restricted to low-life losers you'd never want to know," Young reports. She has counseled several thousand couples over the past seven years at her Center for On-Line Addiction in Bradford, Pennsylvania. Her clientele is loaded with lawyers, doctors, CEOs, and elected officials. "These are people who go to church every Sunday," she says.[3] Cybersex is only one behavior that can destroy great men and ruin marriages. Emotional and physical adultery is becoming common in the workplace and in couple friendships.

Marital researcher Shirley Glass says, "The new infidelity is between people who unwittingly form deep, passionate connections before realizing that they've crossed the line from platonic friendship into romantic love."[4]

Another way we compartmentalize and lead double lives is what we try to do to get a job or influence people. Employers have to double check information on resumes because some people lie. In one part of the interview, they are able to speak truthfully about what they have done and what they would like to do. In another part they lie about their job history. As pointed out, many social scientists believe American culture has actually come to celebrate dishonesty, which encourages lying and cheating in business.[5] Many people mentally shift from truth to untruth without feeling any pain. I talk about this crisis in the next chapter. Compartmentalization leads people like former President Clinton to say and perhaps think that oral sex with an intern isn't really sex. How did he come to that conclusion? How did he permit himself to do that and then have meetings with world leaders or his wife in the same room, five minutes later?

COMPARTMENTALIZATION

But a man who commits adultery lacks judgment; whoever does so destroys himself (Prov. 6:32; NIV).

One of the behaviors that can derail a man's climb to the top is being a "mischievous leader." These people lead by the seat-of-their pants, act on the spur of the moment, and let the chips fall where they may, says David Dotlich and Peter Cairo in their book *Why CEOs Fail*.[6] The authors point out that mischievous leaders are skillful at denying or covering up mistakes. Their eloquence can convince an audience that it wasn't really their fault even though it obviously was. They can deflect attention from themselves by raising another, more compelling issue, arguing over the meaning of words or their true intentions, rather than actual consequences.[7] All of us have seen the bait-and-switch tactic with politicians, coaches, CEOs, and even our own, very smart kids. This struggle of men against moral compromise is as old as Genesis and as current as this morning's *USA Today*. I have conducted ministers' conferences and seminars for businesses and have counseled hundreds of men in cultures around the world, and I find men that fight the same battle of questioning God, vacillate from their dedication to their wife and children, posture themselves for powerful positions, and quit before they reach their goals. This drive within us to succeed, lead, and achieve can trip us up, unless we frequently check our motivations and methods. In trying to find where that line of compromise is, we need to understand — even remind ourselves of some things.

Family patterns. We are being watched and our small children have good hearing. When we are unfaithful, we tend to produce sons who betray their wives and daughters who either accept affairs as normal or are unfaithful themselves.[8]

Biochemical cravings. Changes in brain chemicals during an affair can create a "high that becomes almost addictive," says Atlanta psychiatrist Frank Pittman, author of *Private Lies: Infidelity and the Betrayal of Intimacy*.[9] We can become addicted to a physiological, chemical high while we are emotionally attached to a person we are being unfaithful with. Bonnie Eaker-Weil, author of *Adultery: The Forgivable Sin*,[10] says the biological need for connection can result from "severe stress, loss, or separation" that often can be traced back to childhood.

Internet temptations. Increasing numbers of cyber-affairs are breaking up stable marriages, says psychologist Kimberly Young, author of *Tangled in the Web: Understanding Cybersex From Fantasy to Addiction*.[11] She cites the anonymity and convenience of the Internet, as well as the escape it provides from the stresses of everyday life. Men tend to be visual and, as a result, typically look at photos on the Internet. Women tend to be emotional and so become involved in "chat-rooms." The temptations of the Internet will not go away. The only way to ensure that we will not become involved in this type of pornography is to place boundaries in our lives. Some of the ways I have done this is by giving my password to my wife, my secretary, and the executive team that works for me.

Increasing premarital sex. For years we have known that the more premarital sexual activity a person engages in, the greater the chance of them having an extramarital affair. In fact, "Because girls are more sexually active at younger ages than they used to be, married women are not nearly as inhibited about crossing the line" says Shirley Glass.

Child-centered marriages. Not keeping the relationship alive is a critical error that many couples make. Parents with dual careers and limited time "often collude to give what time they have to the children. Their bond is built on co-parenting, and they don't make time for themselves." Glass says. Stereotypically, in this type of situation the husband finds somebody at work to share his adult interests.

Some affairs happen, Glass says, "because people have certain beliefs they think will protect them. They believe if they love their spouse and have a good marriage, they don't have to worry. They don't exert the caution that might be necessary or create the boundaries to make their marriages safe." Whether it's cybersex, adultery, moving the numbers around in our accounting, "fixing the books," throwing a lie out there, or some other way of crossing the line of good integrity in the middle of our presentation — compartmentalization can fool us into thinking we are okay. Eventually we can get to a point where our conscience doesn't bother us any longer, and that's a very dangerous place.

Knowing the Difference

In the numerous men's conferences, leadership seminars, ministers' retreats, and churches that I've had the privilege of speaking at, I've been with men of many races, nationalities, and economic levels. However, I have seen only three types of men — those who have struggled with compromise and have won, those who still have a daily struggle with compromise, and those who have lost the battle and their lives are in shambles. It doesn't matter if you're a college student, a fast track CEO or CFO, a missionary in the middle of Siberia, or someone who's starting a new business; whoever or wherever you are, you can never totally get away from being tempted. Having the ability to compartmentalize can either allow us to yield to that tempting behavior or we can use it as an advantage to focus, concentrate, and shut off stuff that takes our mental energy. Executives need the ability to block out distractions and focus on the need at hand. Every firefighter has to be able to put his personal issues aside while he saves another person's life. The lawyer must be able to keep his own biases, prejudices, and issues out of the courtroom while he defends his client. The doctor must be able to walk away from handling one emergency patient and go into the next room and do what is correct for a different emergency patient. The pastor or priest must be able to put away a negative comment from a parishioner that comes right before he speaks, and be able to concentrate on the message of the morning. Compartmentalization is a necessary component of leadership. The challenge is to recognize when we are beginning to think about crossing the line of not feeling caution toward a certain behavior that we know is wrong. Following are some ways to recognize that "line in the sand."

Stay honest with your spouse. "Honesty is the trump card for preventing affairs," says Peggy Vaughan, who has studied affairs for more than two decades. Her website is dearpeggy.com. "Make a commitment to sharing your attractions and temptations." This helps us avoid acting on them. Dishonesty and deception cause affairs to flourish, Vaughan says. Keeping secrets from your spouse is not the way to build trust. Our relationship must grow to a level where we are honest, vulnerable, and transparent. I often tell men, "Listen to your wife!" Our wives have an ability to detect the intentions of other women who might be interested in us and can often sense when our hearts are beginning to wander.

"Reveal as much of yourself to one another as possible," Atlanta psychologist Frank Pittman says. "You will find it less necessary to form an intimate friendship with someone else."

Monitor your marriage. "Realize if there is something missing," says psychologist Kimberly Young of St. Bonaventure University in southwest New York state. "Be willing to try to fix it." Assess whether needs are being met. Reading books together, attending marriage retreats, conferences, and seminars are helpful tools for keeping your marriage alive.

Stay alert for temptations. "Be very careful of getting involved in the first place," Young says. "Know the dangers. You can be drawn to an affair as to a drug. And once you are past a certain point of emotional connection, it is very hard to go into reverse." Touching, flirting with the eyes, and sensing that a woman might be available are all behaviors that need to be in check. Counselors understand an emotional issue called "transference." It occurs when a client begins to have an emotional attachment to the counselor. Men need to be aware of transference issues with women on the job, or in the college classroom where they teach or in their congregations. Immediately decide, "Don't go there."

Don't flirt. "That is how affairs start," says Bonnie Eaker Weil, in her website, www.makeupdontbreakup.com. "Flirting is not part of an innocent friendship. If you think there might be a problem with someone you flirt with, there probably is a problem."

Recognize that work can be a danger zone. Emotional attachments can happen quickly. Working with a person of the opposite sex, taking breaks, having lunch, and after work dinners are all areas that we should avoid if possible.

Beware of the lure of the Internet. "Emotional affairs develop quickly in a few days or weeks online, where it might take a year at the office," Young says, "There is safety behind the computer screen." We can disguise our physical appearance, age, income, and location in a romantic liaison on the Internet. We can also develop strong emotional attachments that often lead to adultery. Chat rooms have been proven to be dangerous places for children, also, as sexual predators are always looking for someone vulnerable. A lot of lonely people go there, too. The Internet can help in your research, but can destroy you if you don't place effective screening devices or personal disciplines in place.

Keep old flames from reigniting. "If you value your marriage, think twice about having lunch with one [an old flame]," Glass says. Invite your partner along. I have often told men to throw away old romantic letters from someone other than their wife — gifts or anything that reminds them of what they did with that person when they were physically vulnerable.

Make sure your social network supports marriage. "Surround yourself with happily married friends who don't believe in fooling around," Glass says.[12] The Bible tells us, "Bad company corrupts good character" (1 Cor. 15:33; NIV). If we frequently socialize with couples who question the value of marriage or think an occasional affair is okay, then we will begin to think that they might have a point. Emotions are contagious. When you decide to spend "couple time" with other people who are committed to their marriages and are only interested in their spouse, then it's easier for your commitment to become stronger too.

COMPARTMENTALIZATION

TEMPTATION IS A MENTAL THING

If you are crossing the line, you know that it's difficult to analyze tempta-tion or figure it out logically. It's complicated. Not every temptation falls into a neat, well-defined group. Each bait to compromise has its unique intrigue. Some leaders go to prison for crossing the line, but most men hide their failures and pay the price in a divorce court or with disillusioned children, lost friendships, congregational mistrust, or mental pain. Yet leaders who overcome the temptation to compromise can make an incredible impact on their family, church, company, or school.

Consider 17-year-old Nate Haasis, who broke the passing record for the Central State Eight Conference in Springfield, Illinois. When throwing the record-breaking pass Nate realized that the play might have been a setup. The opposing players simply lined up and watched the snap — not even getting down in a crouch at the line of scrimmage. They made no effort to tackle the receiver. After the fact and after receiving incredible press accolades that he broke the record, he found out what he had suspected. The two opposing coaches had struck a deal in the final minute of play. Nate's team, which had a big lead, would be allowed to score again, uncontested, because Hassis would meet no resistance on the record-breaking pass.

Nate made a decision. He walked away from the record, saying, "I didn't feel right having it." He wrote to the football conference and disowned the record. His rationale? He wrote, "To preserve the integrity and sportsmanship of a great conference for future athletes." Conference administrator Charles Hoots said, "We try to teach honesty, and we try to teach integrity. . . . This is an good example of where a kid steps up and says, 'No, I don't feel right about this, and I want to change this.' "[13]

Nate's comment that he "didn't feel right" shows that his sensitivity is his friend. How would you respond in a similar situation? If you could receive more income by just rearranging the books, would you do it? If you could have an affair and hide it from everyone but yourself and the woman, would you do it? If you could fudge the truth a little on your resume and get a better job as a result, would you do it? Some have developed the ability to compartmentalize so well that they "do it" and really don't feel bad about it. If you're a leader, you will need to compartmentalize. In fact, I believe that everyone does it. Little children do it when they have imaginary friends. As we grow up, we mentally move from imaginary friends to focusing on our jobs, concentrating on mak-ing a good income, and on obtaining material possessions. We have rooms in our mind that hold details of our priorities. Even when we pray, we mentally set some things aside and concentrate on speaking to God. We go into a place of focus on the Lord where God listens and speaks to us about our lives. He talks to us about what is right and what is wrong. He always wants to talk to us, but many decide not to listen. We are sometimes guilty of putting God into another room where we don't hear Him or respond to Him.

If you're putting wrong thinking, emotions, or behavior in a mental room while going on with your life, you could be on the verge of doing something that you will later regret. Many great leaders have done this — for a while. Then they have failed.

Endnotes

1. Karen S. Peterson, "Add to the List of Affairs to Remember," *USA Today* (October 2, 2002): p. 12D.

2. Shirley P. Glass, *Not "Just Friends": Protect Your Relationship from Infidelity and Heal The Trauma of Betrayal* (New York, NY: The Free Press, 2003), p. cover.

3. Peterson, "Add to the List of Affairs to Remember," quoting Kimberly S. Young, *Tangled in the Web: Understanding Cybersex From Fantasy to Addiction* (First Books Library).

4. Karen Peterson, "Infidelity Reaches Beyond Having Sex. Emotional Intimacy, Virtual Affairs Take Hold in Workplace," *USA Today* (January 9, 2003): p. D.08.

5. Joshua Kurlantzick, "Liar, Liar," *Entrepreneur* (October 2003): p. 68.

6. David Dotlich and Peter Cairo, *Why CEOs Fail* (San Francisco, CA: Jossey Bass, 2003), p. 85.

7. Ibid., p. 85–86.

8. Shirley Glass, *Not Just Friends.*

9. Peterson, "Infidelity Reaches Beyond Having Sex."

10. Ibid.

11. Ibid.

12. Ibid.

13. "Bound by Honor," *Winston-Salem Journal*, The Associated Press, November 5, 2003, p. A2.

COMPARTMENTALIZATION

5

EXPECTATION OF SILENCE

Success leaves clues — so does failure. All leaders have people around them who see the clues of integrity, the clues of compromise, or both. We know that, so what do we do if people around us have information about our crossing the line the wrong way? They know what we did.

This creates a dilemma for leaders. If they fire the employee or walk away from the friendship, then the potential of the employee talking is high. But if the leader can do something — give them something or somehow "encourage" them to be quiet — then they can continue doing what they know is outside of the box.

"I'd call it pre-emptive bribery: Treat them well and they won't squeal on you," says Larry Johnson, a consultant and the author of *Absolute Honesty: Building Corporate Culture That Values Straight Talk and Rewards.*[1]

"The CEO realizes he can't promote an extensive fraud without the concurrence of the CFO," says Jonathan Schiff, an accounting professor at Fairleigh Dickinson

> ❧ **THE THINKING IS "BECAUSE OF WHO I AM, PEOPLE WILL PROTECT MY SECRET LIFE."**

University.[2] Professor Schiff also feels the recent stiff penalties and prison time for white-collar criminals is long overdue; however, he said, "It won't fix the core problem of integrity."

Some feel they have the right to expect their peers, employees, or staff to keep their mouth shut when they see or hear something that is out of line — always. It's a loyalty thing. "Sure it's wrong if a rock star takes advantage of an underage girl, but it's considered almost a perk of the job," says Alan Light, the editor of *Tracks* magazine. "Big deal. They mess around, they get drunk, things happen. It can be scandalous, but it's not viewed with the same hostility as same-sex situations."[3]

Then there are buy-offs, examples like the secretary for former Rite Aid executive Franklin C. Brown who said that he wrote her a personal check for $25,000 — after she helped him manufacture backdated documents that qualified him for thousands of shares of stock.[4]

In the Tyco case, the jury heard two former Kozlowski secretaries testify that while having affairs with the CEO they lived cost-free in Tyco apartments. They were later given severance packages and loan payoffs worth hundreds of thousands of dollars.[5]

Switchboard operator and receptionist Tammy Cross said that her bosses made sure she knew to keep quiet about who flew and what was discussed. They also gave the single mother a surprise benefit: college tuition for her daughter.[6]

Kobe Bryant thought that the young woman he decided to have sex with would never tell anyone, because, after all, he was an incredible basketball player.

Michael Jackson thought that his employees would never tell anyone about his interest in young boys. They were well paid and, after all, they had the privilege of working for the "world's greatest rock star."

Whether it is Bernie Ebbers of Worldcom, Dennis Kozlowski of Tyco, or Richard Scrushy of HealthSouth, CEOs often assume their team will remain silent. Many times people have closed their eyes — however, when their neck is on the line, the story comes out.

The expectation of silence is not only a deception many buy into, but it is a huge mistake of many leaders who have lost it all.

WHO IS "REALLY" LOOKING OUT FOR YOU?

All of us need people around us that look out for our good. But those of us who lead need to understand that, from the employee's viewpoint, following requires courage. There is no guarantee that whistle-blowers, or even employees who speak their mind, won't get fired, says David Berg, a psychology professor at Yale University.[7] Is it dangerous to your friends and employees if they tell you something that you "really don't want to hear"? Or, if you are tempted to cross the line of compromise and your employee knows what you are up to and mentions it to you, it can be outright professional suicide for them.

If we don't give people around us permission to talk to us about "yellow lights" of caution, or decisions that they feel are wrong, we could slip into the belief that their silence is part of their job. This viewpoint could eventually hang us. "The lack of great followers is as much to blame as crooked executives for recent scandals. Followers have a duty to speak up — few did," says Brent Longnecker, a Houston corporate governance consultant.[8]

We don't want or need people around us who just mechanically do their work. Every leader needs to give their friends, family, and staff permission to speak up if they see danger, while being loyal to the organization and to us. "Followers don't follow blindly. They have an obligation to strongly express disagreement with the leader, it's also okay for followers to be honest when asked about a decision that they disagree with. It's okay to say that you argued against the policy, but 'it's what we decided to do,' " says, leadership consultant Ram Charan.[9]

I like what entrepreneur and former executive Liz Ryan offers in her "10 pieces of advice to followers" (and leaders) that encourages openness and un-derstanding.

1. Don't take it personally when I'm abrupt. Bosses don't necessarily handle stress any better than anyone else does.

2. I can't make a federal case out of every issue that's important to you. When it comes to doing battle with my own boss or other departments, please let me pick my battles on your behalf.

3. I am not King Solomon. When you and a co-worker both want the desk next to the window, play rock-paper-scissors.

4. Don't give me a reason to watch you like a hawk.

5. You're the expert on how to do your job, not me. Don't be frustrated that I don't know the details. I have a different job description than you do.

6. When you're angry with me, let me know.

7. Don't ask me to tell you what I can't talk about. Are layoffs coming? I like you, but not enough to jeopardize my job.

EXPECTATION OF SILENCE

8. Bring me problems as far in advance as possible. I can help you out of a jam if I have lead-time.

9. Give me feedback on my management style, but be tactful and constructive.

10. I can help you if you goof up, but don't do anything really stupid.[10]

This kind of working relationship fosters honesty, understanding, and integrity. It not only helps the relationships between staff and management, it will help the organization because of increased trust and respect.

Spotting Honest, Loyal People

The Bible tells us about an incredible young man who protected a friend — even when it meant that he could lose the opportunity to be the next king. Saul was the king and Jonathan was his son. Jonathan knew that God had chosen the next person to be king . . . and it wasn't him. God had selected David to be the king because he had an honest heart.

Jonathan and David were close friends. This could have been an awkward situation, in that Jonathan might have chosen to persuade his father to push for him and likely could have gotten most of the country to support him. But, Jonathan had a good heart, too.

Saul had a love/hate relationship with David. On one hand, he needed his military skill (he won the wars); on the other hand, David was a threat to him (he was popular with the people). "The women came out from all the towns of Israel to meet King Saul with singing and dancing, with joyful songs and with tambourines and lutes. As they danced, they sang: 'Saul has slain his thousands, and David his tens of thousands.' Saul was very angry; this refrain galled him" (1 Sam. 18:6–8; NIV). Saul knew his days were numbered. So he tried to kill David more than 30 times.

Jonathan warned David. He told him when his father wanted to kill him. He was more committed to telling the truth and to loyalty than he was to protecting his livelihood — and possibly his own life.

> Then David fled from Naioth at Ramah and went to Jonathan and asked, "What have I done? What is my crime? How have I wronged your father, that he is trying to take my life?"
>
> "Never!" Jonathan replied. "You are not going to die! Look, my father doesn't do anything, great or small, without confiding in me. Why would he hide this from me? It's not so!" (1 Sam. 20:1–2; NIV).

Saul kept trying to kill David, but Jonathan kept David ahead of Saul's wicked plan.

Saul (and Jonathan) eventually lost their lives in a battle. David was a debtor to his friend and tried to honor him after his death by caring for his children.

Among other things, this is a story of letting a friend bring you warning. People want to talk to you when they see danger, caution, or failure. David could have let the fact that he was the next king go to his head. He was the real king, and he had the nation's favor, but David was humble. He wanted other people's advice, wanted to know what was happening back at home, and he listened to his friend. This attitude saved his neck.

There are people in all of our lives who will try to help us; it could be our spouse, children, peers, or staff. But we can choose not to listen and to do the opposite while demanding their "loyal silence." This decision will cause our downfall, just as it did with King Saul. No one dared to warn him of his arrogance.

Tom Peters, author, lecturer, and consultant, reveals that 75 percent of the most recent and innovative inventions came from people outside the profession. Apple Computers, for example, was born in a kid's garage — a kid who left the big boys because they would not listen to him.[11]

> ❧ GIVING FRIENDS, FAMILY, EMPLOYEES, AND PEERS THE PRIVILEGE OF TELLING US THE TRUTH IS A GOOD THING.

Jesus wanted to hear the ideas of His followers. He wanted them to ask questions, make requests, and look for solutions to the concerns that they had. He said, "Keep on asking, and you will be given what you ask for. Keep on looking, and you will find. Keep on knocking, and the door will be opened" (Matt. 7:7;NLT).

Why would the leader want his trainees to ask for what they thought was right, look for solutions, and knock on doors of opportunity? Because He wanted them to know that their ideas, dreams, and goals were valuable gifts.

In the movie *Lawrence of Arabia*, there is a scene of a ten-day march through the desert. The army had thoughts of death because of dehydration as they became more and more lethargic, forcing themselves to go on. They suddenly saw an oasis and submerged themselves in the water. Lawrence counted the men and noticed that one was missing. A camel boy had somehow fallen

EXPECTATION OF SILENCE

off of his camel in the desert. Lawrence told his men, "We must go back and find him." The men were frightened and refused to go, thinking that he would only find the boy dead, and Lawrence himself would risk his life.

Lawrence became frustrated with his men and climbed on his camel and returned to the desert that threatened his life. The men were hopeless and said, "Now we've lost him, too."

Two days later, on the sun-soaked horizon they saw a shimmering figure. "It's Lawrence! He has found the boy!" The men ran to him and Lawrence handed the unconscious boy into their outstretched arms. With a whispering voice of a man who was so thirsty that he could hardly speak, he said, "Remember this: Nothing 'is written' unless you write it." He was saying, "Men, you can go for it, too. Your ideas and dreams are important. Any of you could have done what I did."

LISTENING TO THE VOICE THAT SAYS, "THIS IS WRONG"

"I have a strong sense of right and wrong. If you make truth and honesty lifelong habits, your first reaction will be to do what is right. It's never been as important to me to make other people happy as it is to make God happy," says attorney Mary Walker of Brobeck, Phleger & Harrison, LLP's San Diego Environmental Group.[12]

Walker makes her work count for her clients and, most of all, for God.

She travels all over the United States dealing with disputes over environmental issues. One day she might be working with a biotech firm whose radioactive waste ended up at the wrong site, and another day with an oil company that spilled in a housing area, or she might be involved in a deposition over a pharmaceutical manufacturer whose truck was in an accident and dumped vials of drugs on a highway.

Mary feels that she has a calling to environmental law. This calling has put her in the national spotlight, for example, when she became the head of safety for the nuclear weapons program, three months before Chernobyl. She supervised a team of nuclear scientists sent to Kiev and helped set standards for the United States' nuclear weapons program and nuclear navy.

Excellence and honesty are at the heart of the way she thinks. If a client's problem can be solved by a telephone call, she will do that, even if she could have made more money by getting in deeper. She also has often walked away from requests to change findings of non-compliance in environmental audit reports, because she consistently listens to the voice within.

Her sense of "doing the right thing — no-matter what the cost" has given her the right to speak to government officials, to international environmental decision-makers, to Campus Crusade for Christ events, and to the sixth grade Sunday school class that her son is in.

> Trust in the Lord with all your heart; do not depend on your own understanding. Seek his will in all you do, and he will direct your paths (Prov. 3:5–6; NLT).

TO THINE OWN SELF BE TRUE

One of the most stirring passages in literature is Polonius's advice to Laertes in Shakespeare's *Hamlet*. Laertes has won his father's approval to leave Denmark for France. There seems to be a tug at the old man's heart as he sees the young man eager to go for it and to challenge the future. Perhaps Polonius is bothered by thoughts of when he was young and starting out in life. His advice is full of love and concern that Laertes makes good decisions. "Beware of the entrance to a quarrel," he warns. "Give every man thine ear, but few thy voice; take each man's censure but reserve thy judgment . . . Neither a borrower nor a lender be . . . This above all: *to thine own self be true*, and it shall follow, as the night the day, thou canst not then be false to any man. Farewell; my blessing season this in thee!"

The Bible is a terribly honest book. It doesn't hide the fact that some leaders lied, committed adultery, compromised their convictions, and outrightly deceived people. This book is filled with true stories about real people. God gave us this book to help us understand how to make life work, how to avoid failure in life, and how to get forgiven if we have failed.

Edgar Guest, the poet, wrote:

> I'd rather see a sermon than hear one any day;
> I'd rather one should walk with me than merely tell me the way.
> The eye's a better pupil and more willing than the ear.
> Fine counsel is confusing, but examples always clear,
> And the best of all the preachers are the ones, who live their creeds,
> For to see good put in action is what everybody needs.

One of the biblical leaders that we have not been told of a breech in integrity is Daniel. "But Daniel made up his mind not to defile himself by eating the food and wine given to them by the king. He asked the chief official for permission to eat other things instead. Now God had given the chief official great respect for Daniel. But he was alarmed by Daniel's suggestion. 'My lord the king has ordered that you eat this food and wine,' he said. 'If you become pale and thin compared to the other youths your age, I am afraid the king will have me beheaded for neglecting my duties.' "

EXPECTATION OF SILENCE

Daniel talked it over with the attendant who had been appointed by the chief official to look after Daniel, Hananiah, Mishael, and Azariah. "Test us for ten days on a diet of vegetables and water," Daniel said. "At the end of the ten days, see how we look compared to the other young men who are eating the king's rich food" (Dan. 1:8–13; paraphrased).

Daniel's situation was dangerous, and most would have just gone along with the program. He was taken as a prisoner of war when Nebuchadnezzar conquered Judah in 606 B.C. Nebuchadnezzar was sharp and thought the situation through. He not only took the incredible temple artifacts and treasures, but he kidnapped some of Judah's leaders and young men. This shrewd king might have thought, *If I take the children of the leadership, I'll change their names, re-educate them, train them to speak a new language, and eventually they will think like Babylonians. One day, I'll send them back to their home, Judah, but they will think like me.* He may have thought he could brainwash anyone, if given enough time.

There is no doubt that most of the young people began to adjust and go along with Nebuchadnezzar's tactics. They ate and drank what he gave them. They spoke the language and did well in his university. But not Daniel — or his three friends. They decided to keep their convictions — regardless of the cost. Daniel listened to the voice within. He was true to himself — and true to his God.

Daniel grew as a leader because he listened and didn't pay attention to other people who were compromising.

The most important voice is God's voice, but it is also critical that you listen to the warnings of those around you.

- People around us and those who love us see things that might concern them. They need to have permission to talk to us privately.

- Employees who are loyal to our organization want to be loyal to us. Do they feel that they can bring you problems or issues that they feel cross the line?

- Have you decided to "walk alone" and not do what others are doing in the area of compromise? To do this, you must make your mind up in advance, before the temptation comes.

> ♣ ARROGANCE IS THE FAILURE TO SEE ANY FLAWS. DESPAIR IS THE FAILURE TO ACKNOWLEDGE ANY STRENGTHS.

- Do you understand that every great leader has great temptations? The higher up the ladder you go, the easier target you are.

- Are you content with what God has given you, or do you frequently wish you had what some other leader has?

- Do you pray and try to listen to God's voice? Daniel's strength and confidence came from talking to God every day.

- Do you refuse to be caught by either arrogance or despair?

Plans fail for lack of counsel, but with many advisers they succeed (Prov. 15:22; NIV).

Endnotes

1. "Buying Silence," *Winston Salem Journal*, The Associated Press, January 19, 2004, p. A12.

2. Elliot Blair Smith, "What Puts the CFO in the Middle of Scandals?" *USA Today* (March 4, 2004): p. 1, section B.

3. Donna Freydkin, "Cross the Line?" *USA Today* (December 11, 2003): p. 2D,.

4. Ibid.

5. Ibid.

6. Ibid.

7. *USA Today* (December 10, 2003): p. 2b.

8. Ibid.

9. Ibid.

10. Del Jones, "What Do These 3 Photos Have in Common?" *USA Today* (December 10, 2003): p. 2B.

11. Laurie Beth Jones, *Jesus, CEO* (New York, NY: Hyperion, 1995), p. 188.

12. *Life @ Work*, Fayetteville AR, vol. 3, number 4 (July/August 2000): p. 13.

EXPECTATION OF SILENCE

THE SEX ISSUE — A MAGNET FOR WOMEN

6

We've been exposed to headlines of former President Clinton and Monica, Congressman Gary Condit and his intern, Kobe Bryant and the sexual encounter with a hotel employee, Hugh Grant and the prostitute, Ben Affleck and the Vancouver stripper, R. Kelly and underage girls, Michael Jackson and those child molestation charges, and the never-ending saga of allegations of sexual abuse in the Catholic Church that seems to have involved hundreds more priests than previous estimates suggest (approximately 1,341 priests have been accused of molesting children since the 1950s).[1]

David and Bathsheba, Sampson and Delilah, Lot and his daughters. . . . These events make our heads spin.

Smart, sophisticated men with so much at stake in the office they hold, the position they worked so hard at getting, their career, and their family. Why would these men take the chance? What were they thinking? What would make them risk it all for a few minutes of "???"

She has been the ruin of many; numerous men have been her victims (Prov. 7:26; NLT).

I often remind men who have high profile or important jobs that the ladies around them are not necessarily attracted to their looks, or what they own, but to their power, their influence, their success, and their self confidence. As Atlanta psychiatrist Frank Pittman says, "Certain women are definitely attracted to power. We turn powerful men into sex objects who often have women chasing them. As a rule, men are just not very good at saying no. . . . Affairs are not well-thought out things. They are usually impulsive, even if there is a lot at stake. And that makes it impossible to consider all the ramifications, powerful or not. Those having affairs actually experience a change in brain chemicals akin to a high. The impact is a little like using cocaine. They get a little manic. They think they are bulletproof and that there will be a safety net under them to keep anything bad from happening. And they use grotesque judgment" Pittman says.[2]

Experts feel that the "biochemical craving" kicks in at times of stress, loss, or separation. This high that comes from the encounter can be almost addictive. Many leaders that have become involved in an adulterous encounter have been overtired, stressed out, and/or have a feeling of emptiness.

I have talked to numerous pastors, Christian leaders, and executives who have gotten involved with a woman or with pornography because they felt their "life" was coming back to them. Many were depressed and, for certain, discouraged. Some had been in a burnout depressive mood for months or years. These negative emotions within them caused them to seek a way out, to try to get some energy and excitement back, and as a result they compromised in areas where they never thought they would.

Powerful men have affairs for the same reasons other people do. Those reasons may involve lust, ego building, sensual pleasure, or a lack of something in their marriage, says Weiner Davis, author of *Divorce Remedy: The Proven 7-Step Program for Saving Your Marriage*.[4]

How many are having affairs today? The frequently used percentages indicate that 25 percent of wives and 44 percent of husbands have had extramarital intercourse.

> ❧ I ASK YOU TO PRAY FOR HUMILITY OF ALL OF US. CONGRESSMEN END UP DIVORCING AND MARRYING THEIR CHIEF OF STAFF — BECAUSE THEY ARE "BIG CHEESE."[3]

But a man who commits adultery lacks judgment; whoever does so destroys himself (Prov. 6:32; NIV).

THE VIRTUAL AFFAIR — CYBERSEX

Another form of sexual infidelity is the "virtual affair." This affair of the mind is breaking up stable marriages and ruining careers. People can have a "mental relationship" with someone in the chat room, complete with pictures, and the new thing of virtual encounters allows the user to manipulate the scene to do whatever he desires. I have met with deans of divinity schools, university professors and students, and pastors of great churches who have been involved in "virtual affairs" in their office or on their home computer. Company executives, department heads, and men on the fast track to success have been trapped and sabotaged through this form of mental lust. The anonymity and convenience that the Internet affords is tempting and has made this behavior commonplace. Affairs that take place on the Internet chat rooms are insidious emotional infidelity.

In the new infidelity, affairs do not have to be sexual. Sometimes the greatest betrayals happen without touching. Infidelity is any emotional or sexual intimacy that violates trust, says Shirley Glass, marital researcher.[5]

The job loss of a well-known divinity school dean, a CEO, CFO, executive, pastor, priest, or college professor is now "old news" as this new form of "XXX rated book stores" comes to the family room or office of anyone who has a computer.

Psychologist Kimberly Young, in her book *Tangled in the Web*,[6] says the computer is a tantalizing 21st century "sex toy" that looks benign but can explode like a land mine, erasing the private and work lives of a surprisingly large number of Americans.

Men are more susceptible to Internet pornography and women are more likely to be hurt by e-mail romances (e-romances); 94 percent of men have been exposed to pornography before the age of 20. Exposure to erotica in males before age 14 has at least one significant effect: they are more active sexually and engage in more varied sexual behavior as adults than males not so exposed.[7]

Howard Hendricks, a professor at Dallas Theological Seminary, has studied 237 instances of Christian men (most are Christian leaders) who have experienced moral failure. He found one common factor: not one of the 237 had accountability relationships with other men.

Hendricks asked, "When are you most likely going to face temptation?" Men answered:

THE SEX ISSUE — A MAGNET FOR WOMEN

When you have not spent time with God	81%
When you have not had enough rest	57%
When life is difficult	45%
During times of change	42%
After a significant victory	37%
When life is going smoothly	30%

THE THREE "A's" OF CYBER-SEX ADDICTION

Alvin Cooper, Ph.D., noted researcher on cyber-sex, has described three common reasons men get involved in cyber-sex:

- **Anonymity:** There is a MYTH that when a person goes "online" they are anonymous and nobody can find out who they are, what sites they accessed, or what they viewed/downloaded. This is not true.

- **Accessibility:** Whether you are at home in the privacy of your study, at work in your cubicle, or in the public library "doing research," you can be "just a click away" from . . . whatever. "The Net is the crack cocaine of sex addiction."[8]

- **Affordability:** Cyber-sex is cheaper than paper/print pornography. Often the site will ask for a credit card number when you log on for a "free book" and then ask you if you would like to see more, "hotter, sexier . . . for just $3.95 a minute." And that minute will lead you to another and another.

Cybersex can be more addictive than an actual affair. Daily preoccupation with sex on the Internet becomes an obsession that involves the secret rooms in one's mind. The reason this has so much addictive potential is that it is secret. No other person is involved — just the individual's imagination. A man can go to his highly trained and compartmentalized thinking and literally "be there" with the person he is seeing on the monitor. This secret affair of the mind is so dangerous and hard to let go of because it is . . . so hidden.

WHERE DO YOU WORK?

The workplace can be a sensual zone. As we work more and more hours with the opposite sex, friendships can cross the line. As more women climb the ladder in their professions greater temptations for both sexes increase. "There is a new crisis of infidelity breeding in the workplace," says Baltimore psychologist and marital researcher Shirley Glass. "Often it does not involve sexual thrill seekers, but good people, peers who are in good marriages. The new infidelity is between people who unwittingly form deep, passionate connections before realizing that they've crossed the line from platonic friendship into romantic love."

What is happening? Glass says, three elements are present:

- **Emotional intimacy.** Transgressors share more of their "inner self, frustrations, and triumphs than with their spouses. They are on a slippery slope when they begin sharing the dissatisfaction with their marriage with a co-worker."

- **Secrecy and deception.** They neglect to tell their wife, "We meet every morning for coffee." Once the lying starts, the intimacy shifts further away from the marriage.

- **Sexual chemistry.** Even though the two may not act on the chemistry, there is at least an unacknowledged sexual attraction.[9]

Glass found that 62 percent of the unfaithful men and 46 percent of the women she has treated have met their illicit partner through work.

Run from her! Don't go near the door of her house! (Prov. 5:8).

ARE YOU INVOLVED IN A RELATIONSHIP OR A FRIENDSHIP?

Questions that are included in Glass's book Not "Just Friends" include:

1. Do you confide more about your day to your friend than to your partner?

2. Do you discuss negative feelings or intimate details about your marriage with your friend?

3. Are you open with your partner about the extent of your involvement with your friend?

4. Would you feel comfortable if your partner heard your conversation with your friend?

5. Would you feel comfortable if your partner saw a videotape of your meetings?

6. Are you aware of sexual tensions in this friendship?

7. Do you and your friend touch differently when you're alone than in front of others?

8. Are you in love with your friend?[10]

THE SEX ISSUE — A MAGNET FOR WOMEN

How to Keep Temptation from Getting to You

Be honest with your spouse: Peggy Vaughn says, "Honesty is the trump card for preventing affairs." Make a commitment to share your attractions and temptations. Dishonesty and deception cause affairs to flourish.

Examine your marriage: Ask yourself if there is something missing and be willing to try to fix it.

Daily watch for temptation: Do you feel connected to the person you work with? Is there sexual tension when you are around them? Do you find yourself thinking or daydreaming about them in a sexual way? This can be like a drug that feels good and you can find yourself crossing the line emotionally and find yourself in a compromising conversation or behavior that you cannot reverse.

> Drink water from your own well — share your love only with your wife (Prov. 5:15).

Don't flirt: "That is how affairs start. Flirting is not part of an innocent friendship. If you think there might be a problem with someone you flirt with, there probably is a problem," says Bonnie Eaker Weil, www.makeupdontbreakup.com.

Understand that when you go to work, you could be entering a temptation zone: "Don't lunch or take private coffee breaks with the same person all the time," says Shirley Glass.

The Internet can be your friend — or enemy: You can develop an emotional affair overnight online. I have seen pastors, pastor's wives, executives, students, children, and university department heads who become emotionally involved with someone they have never met, and have sexual conversations that they have never had with people they knew, only to find that if/when they meet the online "friend," the intimacy issues have already been covered, and they quickly jump into bed.

> ❧ I DID SOMETHING FOR THE WORST POSSIBLE REASON, JUST BECAUSE I COULD. I THINK THAT'S JUST ABOUT THE MOST MORALLY INDEFENSIBLE REASON ANYBODY COULD HAVE FOR DOING ANYTHING.
>
> BILL CLINTON[11]

Erase old relationships: "If you value your marriage, think twice about having lunch with one; invite your partner along," says Glass. Better yet, stay away from old flings altogether.

Archibald Hart, psychologist, points out four progressive "red flags" of warning:

Aloneness — when you depend on yourself and are not accountable to anyone

Arrogance — when you believe you know what is right and wrong, but live on the edge

Addiction — when you are preoccupied with sexual thoughts

Adultery — when you act out your thoughts

Work at growing intimacy in your marriage: Being great friends with your wife, and having vulnerable, transparent, and open conversations with her are both parts of developing great intimacy.

Run with people who have good or great marriages: Hang around with couples who love each other and have a growing marriage. Run with people who would never "fool around." There is no question that "bad company corrupts good character."

THREE LEVELS OF INFIDELITY

After speaking at a men's retreat, the corporate executive grabbed my arm and asked if I could speak to him privately. I felt that I had no choice — he was going to talk to me because he felt he needed to. I sensed he was desperate. His eyes were red with strain, tears were running down his cheeks, and, as he began to talk, he trembled. "I had sex with a person that I worked with," he blurted out. "This person was just an employee who worked for one of the supervisors. I had no physical attraction to her and had never even thought about her sexually."

"I was going to the office costume party and needed to change after work. I went into a back room where we stored supplies and was changing my clothes for the party," he explained.

"She walked in the door and I was in my underwear. She didn't hesitate as she walked over to me and just embraced me. Within a minute or two, we were in a passionate frenzy that included intercourse. It was finished in less than five minutes," he said as he paused to catch his breath.

Can a man scoop fire into his lap and not be burned? (Prov. 6:27).

THE SEX ISSUE — A MAGNET FOR WOMEN

"She redressed, turned, and walked out of the room to the party. I stood there in a daze. For months now we have seen each other at work but neither of us has even mentioned the encounter. I have a great marriage. I'm sick because of what I did, and I feel I'll never be able to get over it," was his sad commentary.

What happened? Adulterous encounters come in many packages.

- **The one night stand** — the not-planned-for infidelity — where circumstances, hormones, loneliness, and availability of a partner all affect the outcome.

- **The entangled affair.** It often starts out as a platonic friendship or work relationship. Shared admiration, shared tasks, maybe shared ministry, contribute to developing a friendship that may go on for years, but gradually becomes more romantic than it should. The individuals step beyond the line — they begin to share mutual feelings of attraction with each other. The affair actually starts when the individuals go beyond the line. Physical intimacy is only a short step away.

- **Sexual addiction**: Compulsive sexual activity with various individuals that the perpetrator doesn't even know.

James Dobson, Christian psychologist and founder of *Focus on the Family*, summarizes these three levels with biblical comparisons.

Type 1: The one-night stand typified by David and Bathsheba (2 Sam. 11).
Type 2: The entangled affair similar to Samson and Delilah (Judg. 16).
Type 3: Sexual addiction is illustrated by Eli's sons (1 Sam. 2:22).

THE MAN WHO BEAT THIS TEMPTATION

Do you trust you? It's important that you do and that you think this issue through. You will always have temptations and opportunities to compromise in the sexual area. Billboards, television, videos, the Internet, the gym, and flirty people are not going away. The person you must deal with is you. The only one who can keep you from doing something that can ruin your life is you. You need to make up your mind, plan a defensive strategy before you are tempted, and be willing to walk away from friendships, or even your job, rather than risk moral compromise.

Joseph knew himself, trusted the One who created him, and had a plan on how to escape if he was ever faced with temptation. The Bible explains:

Joseph was a very handsome and well-built man. And about this time, Potiphar's wife began to desire him and invited him to sleep with her. But Joseph refused. "Look," he told her, "my master trusts me with everything in his entire household. No one here has more authority than I do! He has held back nothing from me except you, because you are his wife. How could I ever do such a wicked thing? It would be a great sin against God."

She kept putting pressure on him day after day, but he refused to sleep with her, and he kept out of her way as much as possible. One day, however, no one else was around when he was doing his work inside the house. She came and grabbed him by his shirt, demanding, "Sleep with me!" Joseph tore himself away, but as he did, his shirt came off. She was left holding it as he ran from the house (Gen. 39:6–12; NLT).

What did Joseph do?

He refused. Are you able to refuse the stuff that tempts you — or will eventually tempt you? We need to make up our mind before we have the opportunity. Daydreaming about doing *something* if we have the opportunity is the open door that gives you permission to compromise when the situation happens. We have to make up our mind that when/if the opportunity comes — we will refuse.

He was loyal. He thought of his company, his boss, the one who hired him. He knew his employer had been good to him. He thought of how his behavior would affect his boss. He was loyal to his Creator. He knew that God was good to him and was always there for him. If he compromised, he would be disloyal and that was not what he was willing to do.

He had convictions. All of us have convictions. You have work convictions, rules that you live by, boundaries that you will never cross. Joseph felt it would be wrong. He knew he would disappoint God. He had standards, ethics, convictions, and morals. These are important character qualities for everyone. We are never wrong in developing stronger standards and convictions. It is a way to protect our lives.

He ran. He had safeguards; he knew what he would do. He ran, knowing he could get in trouble for leaving his work. We must mentally decide that nothing will cause us to come to a place where we would compromise — ethically, morally, or with our integrity.

He knew he did the right thing. After the fact, he could look back and not have regrets. He had no shame or guilt and knew that he acted appropriately.

If Joseph would have had a "one night stand" it would have violated his basic character, his convictions, his commitment to his boss, and to himself. He would have been miserable about what he had done to his God.

THE SEX ISSUE — A MAGNET FOR WOMEN

Think about it! The price is HUGE. It's not worth it. You are never wrong doing the right thing.

Say to wisdom, "You are my sister," and call understanding your kinsman; they will keep you from the adulteress, from the wayward wife with her seductive words (Prov. 7:4–5; NIV).

Endnotes

1. Cathy Lynn Grossman, "Survey of Clergy Abuse Cases Suggests Previous Estimates Were Low," *USA Today* (February 1, 2004): p. 2A.

2. Karen Peterson, "Add to the List of Affairs to Remember," *USA Today* (October 2, 2002): p. 12D.

3. While discussing the subject of divorce with a Congressman, I was asked to pray for them and their peers.

4. Peterson, "Add to the List of Affairs to Remember," p. 12D.

5. Karen S. Peterson, "Infidelity Reaches Beyond Having Sex. Emotional Intimacy, Virtual Affairs Take Hold In Workplace," *USA Today* (January 9, 2003): p. D.08.

6. Kimberly S. Young, *Tangled in the Web: Understanding Cybersex from Fantasy to Addiction*, First Books Library, quoted in "Psychologist Untangles the Web of Cyberspace," by Marilyn Elias, *USA Today* (December 12, 2001): p. D.09.

7. Neil M. Malamuth and Edward Donnerstein, editors, *Pornography and Sexual Aggression* (New York: Academic Press, 1984), p. 7.

8. Young, *Tangled in the Web.*

9. Shirley Glass sums up her research in *Not "Just Friends": Protect Your Relationship from Infidelity and Heal the Trauma of Betrayal* (New York: Free Press, 2003).

10. Ibid.

11. Maureen Dowd, "Power Moves: Because They Could, Not Because They Needed To," *New York Times*, quoted in the *Winton-Salem Journal*, June 22, 2004, p. A10.

INTEGRITY

A major U.S. company's chief resigned after authorizing large payments to top executives while negotiating a deal to slash the average worker's pay. A multinational company with significant business in the United States restated its revenue by nearly $1 billion. A leading American firm based in a southern city is charged with massive financial fraud; its CEO, who had lived an extravagant lifestyle, is indicted. It's apparent that despite the 2002 scandals and legislation, little has changed in American business culture. Change appears slow because lying and dishonesty simply have become a much more accepted part of business — and of American life.[1]

Politics, business, and even going to church often have the question mark that asks — is this real? Is this true, or have they fabricated this to look like the real deal? The public's head is spinning with stories of failure, deception, and a sense of "who can I trust?" Many have become "numb" to being shocked by the latest lie.

I once worked for a ministry where the CEO asked me to lie to an employee and fire him for not doing his job — so that the son of the CEO could be hired for the man's position. On another occasion, I was asked by this same person to persuade the board of his organization to give him the $200,000 that they had accumulated in his "key man" insurance policy. Request number one: I said "no" because I would have had to violate my integrity standards in firing a person who was doing his job well. Request number two: I said "no" because I felt it was dishonest, since the money had been paid by the organization to protect *them*, that is, the money was the organization's, not the rightful property of the CEO. On both counts I lost a lot of favor, and soon willingly left the organization.

Compromise of our integrity can come at a high cost:

- Connecticut Governor John Rowland resigned admitting he had made bad choices in accepting gifts from state contractors.

- Hungary's Robert Fazekas, Olympic gold medalist in the men's discus, needed to give the medal back because of doping violations. The 2004 Olympics set a record with more doping violations than ever before. More athletes lied and cheated in order to be in better condition and win — regardless of the cost.

Lee Grady, editor of *Charisma* magazine, recently wrote, "Several national ministries were devastated this year by financial scams. Greedy people who professed to be doing God's work tricked other Christians into investing in a Ponzi scheme — and millions of dollars were lost. The message this sent to the world? Christians can't be trusted. *USA Today*, the nation's largest newspaper, investigated one of its own star reporters and charged him with plagiarizing material and making up stories . . . and the reporter is a born-again Christian. The message this sent to the world? Christians will lie to get ahead. The divorce rate among Christian pastors and leaders today is unprecedented. I know some Bible-believing people who have suddenly thrown everything they ever preached out the window to satisfy a sexual fantasy."[2]

This violation of the "integrity issue" is not only common, but many believe it is part of American life. "Many social scientists believe American culture has actually come to celebrate dishonesty, which encourages lying and cheating in business."[3]

The Center for Academic Integrity at Duke University publishes data on cheating in schools. As you might expect, cheating is on the rise. One study, conducted at nine state universities, asked students about their own cheating. In 1963, 11 percent admitted to cheating; by 1993, nearly half did. In a different study, nearly 80 percent of college students reported cheating at least once.[4]

What causes an honest man to cross the line? Slowly, decisions are made that compromise more and more. The lie that has been thought about in a variety of ways for a long time eventually becomes behavior.

> The man of integrity walks securely, but he who takes crooked
> paths will be found out (Prov. 10:9; NIV).

But, is it worth it? To violate our integrity and injure others causes mistrust, and it will cause others who know us to question what we say. The added danger of losing big time . . . our career, marriage, family, reputation, and more . . . is ever present. Guarding our heart and protecting our integrity are two areas in our lives where we can never compromise. If we do, we need to set it right — ASAP.

Executive coach Stratford Sherman wrote, "The recent scandals are reminders of the need to stop and think and feel. For people willing to grapple with the difficulties of reconsidering integrity, the potential benefits are enormous: the possibility of living with conviction, speaking with credibility, and acting with authority. For business, integrity may not be an immediate moneymaker. The payoff, rather, is long and enduring — reputation, retention of customers and employees, quality of decision-making, and reduced risk of catastrophic misbehavior. For society at large, the potential benefit is a sense of community that derives from shared values, enabling people to live together without suffering the extremes of chaos or oppressive rules."[5]

> When I lay down the reins of this administration, I want to have one friend left. And that friend is inside myself.
> — ABRAHAM LINCOLN

> The integrity of the upright guides them . . . (Prov. 11:3; NIV).

There is an amazing story in the Bible about a couple that co-conspired and decided to lie to God. It seems that they wanted to give the impression to their church that they were being extremely generous in their giving of a piece of property that they owned. The false impression was that they pretended to give all of the money that they sold the property for, but actually they kept some of the money for themselves. The problem wasn't the amount of money they gave. The problem was that they lied. Not just to their pastors and congregational members — but to God. The account in the Bible says, "Ananias, how is it that Satan has so filled your heart that you have lied to the Holy Spirit and have kept for yourself some of the money your received for the land. Didn't it belong to you before it was sold? And after it was sold, wasn't the money at your disposal? What made you think of doing such a thing? You have not lied to men but to God" (Acts 5:3–4; NIV).

The next event might shock you: "When Ananias heard this he fell down and died." A stroke, heart attack, brain hemorrhage — who knows? He died.

The Bible goes on: "About three hours later his wife came in, not knowing what had happened. Peter asked her, 'Tell me, is this the price you and Ananias got for the land?'

" 'Yes,' she said, 'that is the price.'

"Peter said to her, 'How could you agree to test the Spirit of the Lord? Look! The feet of the men who buried your husband are at door, and they will carry you out also.'

"At that moment she fell down at his feet and died" (Acts 5:5–10; NIV).

The people who were watching this occasion were obviously very concerned and might have wondered if they were next. What did God know about them? How did this man named Peter figure out the deception? Would he direct his attention to them next? The Bible says, "Great fear seized the whole church and all who heard about these events" (Acts 5:11).

This event teaches me several things:

1. **Integrity is very important to God.** He is more interested in my heart than my money, my ministry, or even my reputation.

2. **Even Christian people can decide to violate their convictions.** Why? They are people; they struggle like everyone else, and they are tempted.

3. **People are hurt when we compromise truth**. When people see someone get away with compromise they are hurt because they might think, *If they did it and got away with it — then I will too.* I have heard a variation of this many times: "If David (God's man) was able to have an affair and get away with it, so can I." Our mistake, or sin, or bad decision will hurt people. It might be your wife, your son or daughter, your church, or those who secretly watch you, hoping to see someone that will be worth their loyalty.

4. **There is a price to pay when we decide to bend the rules.** The price might be shame, guilt, unfulfillment, or the fear that we will get caught or exposed . . . not to mention, God knows and God remembers.

5. **The purity of the organization (or church) is something we always need to protect**. If a leader compromises, the organization is compromised. If a pastor cheats or rationalizes wrong behavior — the church pays, too.

   Jack Welch said "Integrity is the rock upon which we build our business success — our quality products and services, our forthright relations with customers and suppliers, and ultimately, our winning competitive record. GE's quest for competitive excellence begins and ends with our commitment to ethical conduct."[6]

6. **When someone falls — we should learn from it and let "great fear" seize us.** Some of the greatest "fear" lessons we learn come from watching smart people make stupid mistakes and pay an incredible price for their decisions.

   Wherefore, let him that thinketh he standeth take heed lest he fall (1 Cor. 10:12; KJV).

Lots of CEOs, pastors, leaders, priests, and other men, have gradually let their minds trick them into believing that they will never fall. "Couldn't happen to me — I'm smarter than him," or "I've covered my tracks — put people around me who will protect me."

History records a city named Sardis. The Bible also talks about this city in Revelation 3. Sardis was located very high on top of cliffs and was difficult to get to. Because of its unique location, the citizens believed that their city would never be penetrated or overcome in battle.

The people were basically unafraid of the enemy taking them. They were arrogant, overconfident, and didn't feel they needed to pay attention to details, especially the detail of keeping "one eye open" for invaders. With this attitude, the city fathers didn't take take care of repairing the walls, the foundation, or the major structural pillars of their city. They had become lazy.

The cracks in the walls were not noticed by the leaders. Some of the foundation began to deteriorate. The walls and foundation eventually developed large flaws, which became bigger, deeper, and wider. Many of these openings became wide enough for people to walk through. The people didn't pay much attention and they completely missed the fact that they were no longer safe.

Because of these flaws, it became very easy for the enemy to slip into the city without anyone noticing what was happening.

In the middle of the night, some of their enemies did just that. They climbed the cliff and slipped through the openings in the wall. It happened so quickly — so quietly — while the city was asleep. The invading army located itself in major positions throughout Sardis and aimed their weapons toward all the major spots where the people walked, lived, or where their military might try to protect them.

When the people of Sardis awoke and began their daily routines they were shocked, panicked, and overcome with fear. The enemy was all around them. The city was lost. They had thought they were safe. Sardis — the city that was impossible to beat — lost.

It's easy to begin thinking like the inhabitants of Sardis. Lots of very talented, intelligent, even good people have become complacent. This integrity thing is called character. We are given talent, but we choose to have character.

To protect our integrity, there are some basic life principles that we can follow.

You're never wrong doing the right thing.

All of us have convictions. It's important to embody our convictions and accept the consequences. When we are aware of what is right, we are responsible to do the right thing. Philips Brooks said, "Character may be manifested in the great moments, but it is made in the small ones."[7]

I remember the story of a man named Henry Snowden who drove to a Burger King in Florida. He owned a small business, and during lunchtime he and his friend decided they wanted a sandwich. The manager of the restaurant made a tragic mistake. Inside one of the bags was $4,170 in cash, because the manager was on his way to the bank to make a deposit. The attendant mistakenly handed the bag out the window with the rest of the order.

Snowden thought about the money, the Associated Press reported. "We looked at the money as we ate . . . we knew immediately we should take it back. But I've got to admit, I was definitely tempted."

He returned the money the following morning. The staff, manager, and owner were relieved and full of gratitude. Henry made the right decision. You're never wrong doing the right thing. He valued his integrity more than $4,170.

Do what you say you will do.

Keeping our promises to our family, employees, employers, and churches is basic. This includes being on time, keeping deadlines, and following through with what we said we would do. To be successful with this means that we need to think before we say we will do something. Carefully consider your ability to follow through before you make a promise.

You are responsible for your life.

Demonstrate to people that you understand that you are responsible for every one of your actions. No more seeing other people and outside events as the cause of your problems. Blame no one. Accept the behavior of others and the circumstances of your life as givens, and proceed from there. We are personally responsible. When we see something we don't like, something that needs to be improved, changed, adjusted, or removed, we recognize our personal responsibility to do something about it.

John Maxwell said that as "a leader you have to take responsibility for your own failures as well as successes. That's the only way you'll learn. If you keep learning, you'll improve. If you improve, your leadership will get better. And, in time, you will earn the right to lead on the level you deserve."[8]

Respect people in general.

We can help people live a life of integrity by treating them with respect — even when they do not live up to our expectations. Integrity is contagious — so is compromise. Acknowledge that your own standards are always subject to question. Apologize, and change your behavior when you make a mistake. We will get the best from those around us when there is an atmosphere that supports doing the right thing, one that communicates that you believe they are always capable of making decisions with integrity.

Give yourself an exam — how do you score?

The Bible says; "There is no one righteous, not even one . . . all have sinned and fall short of the glory of God" (Rom. 3:10–23). We are going to make mistakes, over and over throughout life. When we do, we must think about what we did; reflect and ask ourselves *Is this the kind of person I want to be? Is this who I am? Is this mistake (or sin) something that I really need to get some help with?* Examining our life is a good thing. John Maxwell said, "Few things are more dangerous than a leader with an unexamined life."[9]

Write out your rules of integrity and communicate them to those around you.

Executive coach Stratford Sherman said, "Explicit agreement about the basics enables groups of people, from couples to business organizations to nations, to benefit from the integrity of members. Absent consensus, personal integrity can lead dissenting individuals to subvert the group. Among people sharing the same intentions, by contrast, disagreements can help to refine and improve ideas for the benefit of all."[10] The publishing of the rules of integrity for your company, church, or government will set the pace for your organization's ethical standards.

INTEGRITY

Stay on top of your game.

Have you determined that you will be financially sound, pay your bills, watch your spending, and develop a savings plan? Are you protecting your health by watching your weight, trying to stay in physical shape, and visiting your doctor annually for a physical evaluation? Do you work on your marriage and constantly try to improve? You are physical, emotional, spiritual, and relational. It is important that you focus on all of these areas of your life.

> Of those to whom much is given, much is required. And when at some future date the high court of history sits in judgment on each of us, recording whether in our brief span of service we fulfilled our responsibilities — our success or failure, we will be measured by the answers to four questions:
> Were we truly men of courage?
> Were we truly men of judgment?
> Were we truly men of integrity?
> Were we truly men of dedication?[11]
> — John F. Kennedy

Endnotes

1. Joshua Kurlantzick, "Liar, Liar," *Entrepreneur* (October 2003): p. 68.
2. Lee Grady, "A Sober Warning," *Charisma* (May 2004): p. 6.
3. Ibid., p. 70.
4. Stratford Sherman, "Rethinking Integrity," *Leader to Leader* (Spring 2003): p. 42.
5. Ibid., p. 45.
6. John Maxwell, *The Right to Lead* (Nashville, TN: J. Countryman, 2001), p. 100.
7. Ibid., p. 100.
8. Ibid., p. 107.
9. Ibid., p. 105.
10. Sherman, "Rethinking Integrity," p. 45.
11. Maxwell, *Right to Lead*, p. 111.

ANGER

8

O ut of control — anger overrules our reasoning process and can cause us to do what we thought we would never do.

Anger is an interesting thing to study. Why some seem to control it and others lose it is often influenced by what's going on between the ears. A leader can calmly handle pressures, decisions, and intense challenges for months or years, but one day blow up and do a lot of damage — sometimes so much damage that it can't be repaired. I think those of us who have a lot of responsibility, have experienced times when we could have lost control — or when we actually did. When that happens, we think back, *If only I would have handled it differently.*

Moses was perhaps one of the world's greatest leaders. He was groomed from the beginning of his life to lead. The best in upbringing, education, and "internships" prepared him to lead in ways that he didn't expect. Most experts believe that Moses led an Israelite community of at least three million people. He was exceptional; he accomplished much, and his name has been referred to around the world for about 3,500 years — regardless of the speaker's religious background. However, one day the pressure got to him and he "lost" it. His anger and disappointment with the constant criticism from people he was leading, boiled to the point where he exploded. Forty years earlier he had killed a man. That was terribly wrong — however, the murder was not out of anger. Then, he wanted to defend a fellow Israelite. He was young, full of zeal, and the desperate desire to help his people drove him to intervene in a physical confrontation that he walked up on — and he took a person's life. Because of that act, Moses ran into the wilderness and thought about what he had done for 40 years.

This day, however, he was ticked off. He had heard the complaints, the gripes, and the ingratitude for long enough. As the leader of millions of people, he was responsible for directing them to a place where they could have a life without slavery. The complaints were daily. He needed to learn the skill of delegation and empowerment. But instead of organizing a team of leaders around him to deal with the customer complaints, he carried the weight himself. The weight was too much and he literally had a temper tantrum in front of the people. He was their leader. And leaders are supposed to keep their emotions under control . . . at least that's what we think and hope.

The people were complaining and being ridiculous. They said, "Why did you bring us up out of Egypt to this terrible place?" (Num. 20:5; NIV).

Moses must have thought, *Don't they remember their pain, their slavery, their poverty?*

They had the opportunity for a new start. It was like they were moving from Haiti to America. *Why can't they be grateful, see what I see, get the big picture?*

The Bible tells us that "The Lord said to Moses, 'Take the staff, and you and your brother Aaron gather the assembly together. Speak to that rock before their eyes and it will pour out its water' " (Num. 20:7–8; NIV).

Moses had had this experience before. On another occasion, he was hearing the same complaints, and the Lord gave him *different* instructions. "I will stand before you by the rock at Horeb. Strike the rock, and water will come out of it for the people to drink" (Exod. 17:6; NIV). But this time, Moses was mad, not just stressed out. Moses and Aaron decided to take matters into their own hands. "He and Aaron gathered the assembly together in front of the rock and Moses said to them, 'Listen, you rebels, must we bring you water out of this rock?' Then Moses raised his arm and struck the rock twice with his staff. Water gushed out, and the community and their livestock drank" (Num. 20:10–11; NIV). Speak, strike, what's the difference? What's the big deal?

The big deal is, Moses was out of control the second time. He yelled at the people and he hit the rock — twice. Speaking and yelling are two different things. He also labeled them instead of leading them by example. Regardless of what they were doing, he was wrong. Demonstrating to the people that he didn't have it together wasn't the example God wanted him to be.

The price?

The Israelite community eventually got to go into the place called "a land flowing with milk and honey" — the land of Canaan — but Moses and Aaron didn't.

> The Lord said to Moses and Aaron. "Because you did not trust in me enough to honor me as holy in the sight of the Israelites, you will not bring this community into the land I give them" (Num. 20:12).

When Moses "struck" instead of "spoke," he fell — because he let his anger get to him. As leaders, we can let the job, the people, or the hours get to us. But we set ourselves up for failure.

> A fool gives full vent to his anger, but a wise man keeps himself under control (Prov. 29:11).

Another great leader did a similar thing. George Sweeting described the difficulty Alexander the Great experienced trying to control his temper. "On one occasion, Cletus, a childhood friend and general in his army, became intoxicated and ridiculed the emperor in front of his men. Blinded by anger, Alexander snatched a spear and hurled it at Cletus. Although he had intended only to scare the drunken general, the spear took his friend's life."[1] Alexander was able to conquer many nations, but he was unable to control his own anger.

MEN AND TESTOSTERONE

Moses, Alexander the Great, and Indiana Pacer basketball star Ron Artest have one thing in common — testosterone. These men had incredible talent but didn't control their emotions. What did Ron Artest pay for his huge outburst of anger? Seventy-three basketball games, which equaled 4.99 MILLION DOLLARS. So someone yelled at him, called him a name, threw a glass of beer on him. Was a moment of "payback" worth almost $5 million?

Other players became involved, too. Stephen Jackson of Indiana lost 30 games equaling $1.63 million; Jermaine O'Neal of Indiana lost 25 games equaling $4.11 million; Anthony Johnson of Indiana lost 5 games at

ANGER

$133,333; Ben Wallace of the Detroit Pistons lost 6 games equaling $400 thousand; and Reggie Miller of Indiana, and Elden Campbell, Chauncey Billups, and Derrick Coleman, all of Detroit, were all fined games and thousands of dollars. Men generally handle anger differently than women. We have found that brain differences between the sexes can lead men and women to view anger-producing situations with different mindsets. These same brain differences can predispose men and women to choose certain responses to anger rather than others.[2]

Higher male hormonal levels are implicated in male aggressiveness and more overt expressions of anger. Men have ten times the level of testosterone in their bodies than women have. Both men and women get angry, but the flood of testosterone in the male pushes harder against men toward certain anger expressions. Men and women both use verbal expression, but men overwhelmingly choose physical violence. This does not mean that higher levels of testosterone dictate anger responses.[3]

It seems that men and women are wired differently, and because of this men choose to act inappropriately more often. Letting the adrenaline rush get to them and choosing to raise their voice, to label, to cuss, or to become physical is often the choice a man makes. Aggression is something that is permitted from childhood on and "losing it" is somehow permitted in boys and men. More men have gotten into trouble because of their verbal choices, or their decision to physically take matters into their own hands. However, it doesn't have to be that way. A man's chemical make-up can also help us deal with difficult leadership issues with energy and creativity.

THE CULTURE

From early childhood, our culture gives males permission to be more aggressive than women with their anger. Women learn how to manage it differently. We expect little girls to be good and calm and to never lose control. With males, aggressive behavior is tolerated and at times encouraged. After the age of three — when little boys begin to kick and hit with more frequency — little girls begin to use more verbal insults and facial expressions such as rolling their eyes, curling their lips, and sticking out their tongues. Boys are quite capable of verbal aggression, but boys shout with their bodies as well as their mouths.[4]

THE EXAMPLE

Studies of the effects of father absence in the lives of adolescents show a significantly higher rate of delinquent behavior and a much higher incidence of violence. Between 85 and 90 percent of adult male prisoners were raised in fatherless homes or in homes with violent, abusive fathers. The percentage for adult female prisoners is almost as high.

Psychologist and author David Stoop tells of a man who didn't want to lose his temper like his father. However, he ended up losing it — in a different way. Terry was a 40-year old commercial artist, who came to counseling because his wife was concerned about his "anger problem." He was quick to point out that he never got angry with her — that wasn't the problem. He simply got angry at everything else. If he was working on a layout and the lead in his pencil broke, it was hard to tell what would happen next. If it was a good day, it might take several pencil breaks before he lost control. If it was a bad day, the first time the lead broke he would erupt with a rage, sometimes even tearing up the design he'd been working on.

If he was working on a project around the house, the minute the slightest thing went wrong, he would lose it, sometimes causing enough damage that a workman would have to be called to fix not only the original problem, but also the additional damage Terry had caused in his anger.

The final straw came when he and his wife were driving somewhere and an older driver did something that sent Terry into a rage. He chased the other car, and at a traffic light he actually got out of the car and was prepared to pick a fight with a man old enough to be his father.

Even though Terry said he never got angry with his wife, it's easy to imagine how his anger directly affected his marriage relationship. His wife was often either embarrassed or frightened, or both, but now she was also fed up with his "anger problem."[5]

Dr. Stoop found out that since Terry's dad didn't know how to handle his own anger, he couldn't teach his son about controlling anger. Terry grew up with a father who often lost control. He felt it was safe to lose control with an inanimate object and not with a real person. But that eventually happened as well. As a result, he almost lost his marriage.

> Don't sin by letting anger gain control over you. Don't let the sun go down while you are still angry (Eph. 4:26; NLT).

LEADERS KNOW ANGER

All leaders experience anger; in fact, everyone does. The unique pressures of responsibility, managing people, and making huge decisions add to the pressure that "those in charge" feel. Pressure goes with the territory. Hard decisions are part of the job, and difficult people are in every occupation or church. Those who decide to take on added responsibility also decide to deal with different personalities, more complicated situations, and higher risks. Moses,

ANGER

David, George W. Bush, Bill Gates, and every other leader understands this up front — or soon gets it. Pastors, principals, CEOs, and upper management people will adapt to this or eventually decide not to lead at that level. The Bible tells us that anger can be controlled and that we can put a time limit on it (see Eph. 4:26). The problem is that many think the opposite. They think or have been taught that out-of-control anger never ends. Not true. Your leadership "grade" largely depends on how you control your emotions — *anger is an emotion.*

Pray like this . . . forgive us our sins, just as we have forgiven those who have sinned against us (Matt. 6:9–12; NLT).

LEADERS KNOW THE IMPORTANCE OF FORGIVENESS

Leaders are to understand and demonstrate forgiveness. Most anger comes from hurt, disappointment, or frustration. We become hurt because of what someone said. The criticism that Defense Secretary Donald Rumsfeld received with his decisions in Iraq saddened him. "I am truly saddened by the thought that anyone could have the impression that I or others here are doing anything other than working urgently to see that the lives of the fighting men and women are protected and cared for in every way humanly possible."[6] His job could never have 100 percent approval — doubtful it would have 60 percent, and at times would have less than 50 percent. He knew that, coming into the job. People will criticize you — and it will hurt. A tough hide with a tender heart is a goal that leaders must have.

> ❧ ANGER IS ALWAYS DIRECTED AGAINST INDIVIDUALS . . . BECAUSE THAT PERSON HAS DONE OR MEANT TO DO SOMETHING AGAINST HIM.
> — ARISTOTLE[7]

People will disappoint us and sometimes follow their own set of rules. Remember, we have disappointed people before, too. We all have feet of clay; we have all made mistakes and we are all in a continual growing process. Choosing not to forgive injures us more than them. In his Bible study guide, Charles Swindoll wrote, "From a worldly perspective, it may be quite rational and justifiable to hold onto anger and bitterness. After all, one may reason: that person doesn't deserve forgiveness. However, the burden brought about by another person's harmful actions often inflicts more pain on the one who needs to forgive than on the one who needs to be forgiven . . . the acid of resentment and hate eating away at [one's] peace and calmness."[8]

We can become frustrated by them or with ourselves. Not reaching our goals and objectives in our time is frustrating; however, all goals are not reached, our sense of timing is sometimes off because of unknown factors, and daily we need to re-evaluate our timelines and objectives. Forgiving others and forgiving ourselves, while at the same time being a responsible leader, is a balance that changes every day. We never know what a day may bring, however, we can control how we feel about it. Leaders have great responsibility — and are to have great discipline over their emotions.

Our sense of power can get out of control, that is, the sense of entitlement. When we think we have a right to lose control, say what we want, or decide without thinking, this attitude is often driven by the idea that "we have a right, because of who we are." We can abuse our power when we are frustrated, discouraged, or when other people do not respond in the way we thought they should. We can justify our anger and our "acting out" as the natural consequences of being misunderstood or someone's disagreement with how we do things. Our sense of "entitlement" can make us feel that we have a right to redefine others. The danger? We think we can control others by putting them down with words, attitudes, and actions. This belief will block our ability to learn from others and to be open to new ideas. Some of the greatest gifts we have are the other people God has put in our paths or allowed us to lead. The entitlement thing can greatly injure our ability to learn from others and encourage them to contribute to the organization we serve.

Angry at life, Jonah didn't like his assignment. He was given a job that he didn't want. He became angry at the idea of following through on what he was asked to do. He was a prophet to the nation of Israel. He liked the prophet job, but not this particular assignment. God asked him to go to the Ninevites. "Get up and go to the great city of Nineveh! Announce my judgment against it because I have seen how wicked its people are" (Jon. 1:2; NLT). These people had tortured, plundered, and killed his fellow Israelites. They deserved to die. Jonah wanted them to be punished — eliminated. He took matters into his own hands and decided that they didn't deserve a warning of God's impending judgment. Jonah ran away from his responsibility, and he ended up getting into a frightening, miserable condition. When he was in rebellion, he changed his mind. He decided to do what God asked him to. The Ninevites repented of their sin and God forgave them and held back His judgment. This greatly angered Jonah. "When God saw that they had put a stop to their evil ways, he had mercy on them and didn't carry out the destruction he had threatened. This change of plans upset Jonah, and he became very angry" (Jon. 3:10–4:1; NLT).

Jonah's anger put him in a downward emotional spiral that eventually caused a deep depression. He said, "Death is certainly better than this!"

God said to Jonah, "Is it right for you to be angry?"

"Yes," Jonah retorted, "Even angry enough to die!" (Jon. 4:3–9; NLT).

Lots of leaders become angry at their job or what they are required to do. This anger can take the fun out of life, cause your marriage to be harmed, and put you into a deep depression. I have met many company leaders, managers, pastors, and department heads who are very angry and unhappy with their jobs. The position has gotten to them, the assignment isn't what they thought it would be, and the pressure has beat them down. Some continue to stay on the job for the money, hold steady until retirement, or they don't know what else they would do. What many don't realize is that there are parts of *all jobs* that we won't like. There will always be things that we are required to do that we don't agree with. As long as it isn't unethical, illegal, or a violation of our conscience, we need to accept this part of the job along with the parts we like.

God knew best. In Jonah's situation, Jonah knew that God would forgive the Ninevites. "That's why I ran away ... I knew that you were a gracious compassionate God, slow to get angry and filled with unfailing mercy. I knew how easily you would cancel your plans for destroying these people" (Jon. 4:2; NLT).

As leaders it is common to be in situations that we don't like. This can greatly injure our ability to have peace and contentment. Throughout history, great leaders have found a way to do the difficult parts of their job and maintain a sense of emotional balance. In every business or church there are written and unwritten rules. Doing our jobs with excellence and a sense of loyalty will help us find balance.

UNDER CONTROL

By all reports, Martin Luther King Jr. was a gentle man, but surely his anger over injustice energized and motivated him to lead the civil rights movement that changed America for the better. When Jesus saw that the temple was being used for a business, He overturned the tables and benches, stopped people from carrying merchandise through the temple courts, and accused them of turning God's house of prayer into a den for robbers (Mark 11:15–17). He had righteous, controlled anger that challenged the religious leaders toward doing the right thing.

When Jesus saw a man who had a deformed hand, He decided to heal him. He had people all around Him who questioned His right to heal on the

Sabbath. He looked at His critics with righteous indignation (anger) and did the right thing (Mark 3:1–5). He healed the man on the Sabbath. A basic form of anger is necessary for survival and is normal. It can serve as a motivator for settling interpersonal conflicts, can give us a better sense of timing during pressure and stress, and can be controlled. "Be quick to listen, slow to speak, and slow to become angry" (James 1:19; NIV). Anger should be recognized as an emotion that can be used for our good — then, let it go.

HOW TO FIND THE BALANCE

- Acknowledge anger when you feel it and think about why you are feeling angry. It probably isn't possible to get rid of anger or bitterness if you deny that you have it. Control what you say, what you do, and what you react to inappropriately by thinking about how to respond in the right way. "The godly think before speaking; the wicked spout evil words" (Prov. 15:28; NLT).

- Take the high road. Decide not to take revenge. Revenge is something we can leave in the hands of our Creator. The attitude of having to repay people when they hurt us or speak against us will destroy us. We have all been hurt. All of us have our war stories. Don't carry these experiences around and let the memories eat at you. Give them to the one who knows everyone's motivations and actions. Let Him deal with the person or situation. Confess your anger to God and tell others when you were wrongfully angry with them. Admit it. God will forgive you and most of the time, people will. Sincerely asking them to forgive you is the key. In turn, forgive them for what they have done to you (sometimes repeatedly).

- Understand that there are right ways and wrong ways to express anger. When we need to confront, correct, or evaluate wrong behavior, controlled anger is valid. But always try to combine it with encouragement, patience, and careful instruction.

Endnotes

1. G. Sweeting. "Climbing Higher: Temper, Temper," *Moody Magazine* 93 (7) 1003: 74.

2. Anne Moir and David Jessel, *Brain Sex* (New York: Dell Publishing Group, Inc., 1991), p. 68–87.

3. Natalie Angier, *Woman: An Intimate Geography* (New York: Hougton Mifflin Co., 1999), p. 238–262.

4. Mark Cosgrove, *Counseling for Anger* (Dallas, TX: Word Publishing 1988), p. 73–104.

5. David Stoop, Ph.D., *Christian Counseling Today*, vol. 8 no. 2 (2000): p. 21.

ANGER

6. Defense Secretary Donald Rumsfield during a press conference on December 22, 2004.

7. Lane Cooper, translator, *The Rhetoric of Aristotle* (New York, London: D. Appleton and Company, 1932), p. 93.

8. C.S. Swindoll, *Koinonia: A Recipe for Authentic Fellowship, Bible Study Guide* (Dallas, TX: Word Publishing, 1995), p. 44.

9

ACCOUNTABILITY — EGOS IN CHECK

PLANS FAIL FOR LACK OF
COUNSEL, BUT WITH MANY
ADVISERS THEY SUCCEED
(PROV. 15:22).

The higher up the leadership ladder we go, the easier target we are. The more responsibility we have, the more we need good advice. The advice, counsel, and accountability that we choose to include in our decisions provides us with a greater ability to hit the right target.

A lot of leaders' "egos" don't like accountability. It presses in on their sense of pride — it challenges their desire to be in front — and this aversion has caused a lot of great leaders to make bad decisions.

While attending the 2005 National Prayer Breakfast in Washington D.C., I sat with a congressman and we discussed how power can sometimes tempt leaders to make bad decisions. The six-term congressman said, "Ours is a place where people make decisions for all the wrong reasons. We need prayer that we'll make decisions for the right reasons." I was then informed that they believed that there were more "accountability" and "Bible study" groups going on in the Senate and in the Congress than they could remember.

Do not be wise in your own eyes (Prov. 3:7; NIV).

Colin Powell has headed armies and government agencies and has been the U.S. Secretary of State. He is a world leader with strong opinions. He has a "code of leadership" that guides him in a sea of decisions. He has an opinion about what leaders have to do to consistently get the "right" information — not just the information they "want."

His *seven laws of power* build around him a protection boundary that has saved him from wrong choices many times.[1] They include:

1. Dare to be the skunk. "Every organization," says Powelll, "should tolerate rebels who tell the emperor he has no clothes . . . and this particular emperor expects to be told when he is naked." Powell is a gentleman. He's not rude or mean. As a good leader, he patiently builds a consensus, by prodding people while simultaneously listening, learning, and involving them. But, he admits, he understands that being responsible with the accurate information sometimes means making strong leaders angry.

We don't like information that challenges what we feel we want to do but it is critical that we receive the right information from the right people.

2. To get the real dirt, head for the trenches. "The people in the field are closest to the problem, therefore that is where the real wisdom is." On the eve of the Desert Storm campaign, Powell solicited enlisted men and women for advice on winning the war.

"When a captain came to see me, I would tell him to sit down and say, 'Talk to me, son. What have you got?' And then I'd let him argue with me, as if he were arguing with an equal. After all, he knew more about the subject than I did. I also knew he would tell his friends that he had argued with the Chairman of the Joint Chiefs of Staff. Word would spread, and people would understand that when they came into my office I really wanted to hear what they thought." He trusted their opinions.

Lucent Technologies CEO Patricia Russo said, "A winning team is not people who salute and march down the path. The closer you get to the customer, the more you know about where the opportunities are. All good ideas are not in the headquarters of corporations."[2]

Leaders who ask for straight talk from the trenches must graciously accept information and diverse opinions—even ideas they don't want to hear. "The day soldiers stop bringing you their problems is the day you have stopped leading them," says Powell.

The further you get from the custodian, support staff, and laity, the further you get from reality. We need to protect ourselves from being bombarded with negative information; however, in this process we often remove ourselves from reality.

3. Share the power. "Plans don't accomplish work," says Powell. "It is people who get things done." He adheres to two basic leadership premises: 1) people are competent, and 2) every job is important.

"Everybody has a vital role to play," he told the State Department staff when he took over as secretary, "and it is my job to convey down through every layer to the last person in the organization the valuable role they perform."

The leadership philosophy of TEAM is also a commitment to accountability — and an "ego" check. We simply need every member of the team to do their job or else our mission, our lives, and the organization won't work. The TEAM needs to feel that we need them; otherwise, the church, company, or government agency will not work like it should. How we communicate "thank you's" and encouragement is critical to the process.

4. Know when to ignore your advisers. Experts, advisers, opinions, coaches, and consultants will only get you so far. Eventually a leader must make the final decisions.

The longer you lead, the more you can trust your "gut feeling." After you have received all the critical information you need, you have a decision to make. It's your decision.

Powell says; "Experts often possess more data than judgment, elites can become so inbred that they produce hemophiliacs who bleed to death as soon as they are nicked by the real world."

The best leaders, he believes, should never ignore their own hard-won experience. While we are to "crave" good advice, we must trust our instincts to call the shots. Good information, experience, a sense of "this is the right thing to do," and a gut feeling are all part of making right decisions. When we make a mistake, we regroup, make it right, and admit that we were off. Then correct the direction in which we are going.

5. Develop selective amnesia. Too many leaders get so trapped in fixed ways of seeing things that they can't cope when the world changes. Powell says,

"Never let ego get so close to your position that when your position goes, your ego goes with it."

Life changes constantly. Hold on to your position *lightly;* however, keep your sense of positive self-esteem *tightly.* Many leaders fight until death when the company decides to downsize, relocate, or reengineer. In a few months or years, they destroy their reputation, and injure their families and their health over a "job." Leaders are leaders. If you can't lead where you are, lead somewhere else.

6. Come up for air. Powell demands excellence from his staff, but also insists they have lives outside the office. He told his State Department staff, "If I'm looking for you at 7:30 at night and you are not in your office, I'll consider you a wise person. Anybody who is logging hours to impress me, you are wasting time."

I have come that they may have life ([Jesus] John 10:10; NIV).

Many great leaders have made disastrous decisions when they were too tired or burned out. Your time off — day off, evenings, vacation, time blocked out for focus, etc. — is time that you will get more energy to do what you need to do. Some leaders feel that free time is their enemy. They are driven to continue doing and developing but miss the necessity of resting and receiving energy and getting in touch with their creativity.

Good advice: get a life. Every leader needs to have a "Camp David."

7. Declare victory and quit. "Command is lonely," says Powell. And so is the decision to withdraw from the position of authority — a choice he says not every leader makes soon enough. His own retirement from the military was, in his word, "traumatic."

"One of the saddest figures in all of Christendom," he says, "is the Chairman of the Joint Chiefs of Staff, once removed, driving around with a baseball cap pulled over his eyes, making his strategic choice as to whether it's going to be McDonald's or Taco Bell."

"Leadership," he says, "is not rank, privilege, titles, or money. It's responsibility."

Knowing when enough is enough, the project is finished, the task is complete, and it's time to pack, is a sensitivity that all leaders must acquire. Pushing it over the edge doesn't help anyone or any organization. You have done your job; the mission is complete and God has enabled you to bring the church or

❧ SOME LEADERS DON'T LIKE TO LISTEN TO GOOD ADVICE.

organization to another level. As Powell says, "Declare victory and quit." You have a life beyond the job. It's another job, project, goal, and dream that you have been thinking about.

A wise man listens to advice (Prov. 12:15; NIV).

Another military leader was a man named Naaman. The Bible tells us, "He was a valiant soldier" (2 Kings 5:1; NIV).

Though he was a great military leader, he refused to listen to God's advice about how to deal with a problem. As a result, his physical challenge of leprosy prevented him from going into the public and enjoying his life more fully. His ego problem kept him from the very thing he wanted and hindered his ability to lead. This common problem with leaders *takes — rather than gives* — what they want.

> ❧ PEOPLE AREN'T REALLY LIKE THAT — THE OFFICE MAKES HIM LIKE THAT.[3]

A young girl from Israel who served Naaman's wife told her, "If only my master would see the prophet who is in Samaria! He would cure him of his leprosy" (2 Kings 5:3; NIV). The prophet was a man named Elisha.

The Bible tells us, "So Naaman went with his horses and chariots and stopped at the door of Elisha's house. Elisha sent a messenger to say to him, 'Go, wash yourself seven times in the Jordan, and your flesh will be restored and you will be cleansed.' "

"But Naaman went away angry and said, 'I thought that he would surely come out to me and stand and call on the name of the Lord his God, wave his hand over the spot and cure me of my leprosy. Are not Abana and Pharpar, the rivers of Damascus, better than any of the waters of Israel? Couldn't I wash in them and be cleansed?' So he turned and went off in a rage."

The leader Naaman had his own idea about how his healing should take place. His ego was strong; he had a sense of pride that almost kept him from getting what he needed. He was ready to walk off. His idea of how it should be done almost ruined the possibility of a miracle.

You might be there right now. Or, you might know of a leader who is stuck on their own "Harvard University" idea. It is textbook, it is my idea, and it is right, by golly.

This attitude has taken the "life" out of many men. It's "macho" but it can kill you.

"Naaman's servants went to him and said, 'My father, if the prophet had told you to do some great thing, would you not have done it? How much more, then, when he tells you to wash and be cleansed!' So he went down and dipped himself in the Jordan seven times, as the man of God had told him, and his flesh was restored and became clean like that of a young boy" (2 Kings 5:9–14).

Naaman was a strong leader. He obviously did a very wise thing in surrounding himself with people to whom he was willing to listen. These people could speak up and disagree with him, and they gave him excellent advice. Naaman changed his mind, followed the prophet's instructions, and as a result, his leprosy was healed. Leaders who are accountable and listen to instruction receive ongoing success.

To keep the ego in check, many times you will need to listen to people you don't want to listen to. God knows how to balance healthy ego and unhealthy pride.

> Pride only breeds quarrels, but wisdom is found in those who take advice (Prov. 13:10; NIV).

HOW MUCH DOES PEOPLE'S SILENCE COST YOU?

Surrounding yourself with "yes men" will not help you see the real picture either. Some leaders choose to buy the silence of people who know the other side of the story. Dennis Kozlowski, former Tyco chief, did and many CEOs, CFOs, executives, and some television evangelists and religious leaders have.

The pattern that seems to run through white-collar crimes is that executives ply their underlings with expensive gifts and other unexpected perks. Experts on corporate practices contend that the real purpose (of that practice) was to buy the support staff members' loyalty — and silence — and the higher-ups sought to evade regulators. "Treat them well and they won't squeal on you," said Larry Johnson, a consultant and author of *Absolute Honesty: Building Corporate Culture that Values Straight Talk and Rewards Integrity*.[4]

> Good leaders cultivate honest speech; they love advisors who tell them the truth (Prov. 16:13; The Message).

John Maxwell said good team leaders never want yes-men. They need direct and honest communication from their people. He says, "I have always encouraged people on my team to speak openly and directly with me. Our meetings are often brainstorming sessions where the best idea wins. Often, a team member's remarks or observations really help the team. Sometimes we disagree. That's okay, because we've developed strong enough relationships that we can survive conflict. Getting everything out on the table always improves the team. The one thing I never want to hear from a teammate is, 'I could have told you that wouldn't work.' "[5]

Accountability is a trust relationship with someone where confidentiality, honesty, and loyalty are foundational. Being willing to listen to others and let them speak into our lives is a critical attitude leaders must have. It is not weakness to get good advice — it is strength to seek it out.

But pity the man who falls and has no one to help him up (Eccles. 4:10; NIV).

Why do leaders derail? One said, "He didn't have any fences in his life — safety measures." Another said, "He could not believe it was possible that he would fail." When a broken leader was asked what he felt was the reason for his fall, he said, "I didn't give anyone permission to tell me about my blind spots, I only gave them permission to tell me what I wanted to hear." One pastor said, "I didn't listen to my wife."

EGO CAN PREVENT YOU FROM HEARING WHAT YOU NEED TO HEAR

All leaders are busy — accountability takes time. Accountability is often viewed as something negative, to be avoided at all costs. However, it is actually a blessing for those willing to submit to it. To be accountable means that we are willing to be responsible to another person for our behavior and it implies a level of submission to another's opinions and viewpoints.

It is dangerous for anyone to live without accountability. Ted Engstrom said, "An unaccountable spouse is living on the edge of risk; an unaccountable CEO is in danger of taking his company down a wrong road; an unaccountable pastor has too much authority; an unaccountable counselor has too much responsibility and needs too much wisdom to be able to handle it on his own."[6]

Wounds from a friend can be trusted (Prov. 27:6).

Our wives can be the greatest accountability partners we have. Many couples have jobs that require them to be away from home. This can be dangerous, stressful, and can challenge the stability of the best of marriages. Dennis Rainey, executive director of Family Life Ministry follows these guidelines:

- Go over schedules weekly to minimize surprises. Anger can boil if a spouse was counting on the other and he or she's gone — again! Include children in the schedule discussions so that they know what's coming.

- Discuss communication expectations. With e-mail and cellular phones, connect several times each day when apart.

- If possible, set limits on the number of nights you'll be away — per trip and annually.

- Discuss expectations and needs of both the road warrior and the non-traveler when both are home. Record a reminder of your spouse's list in your Palm Pilot or computer.

- Leave some margin in the home schedule for emergency business travel.

- Make needed adjustments together when you over-schedule travel. We do make mistakes. The issue is whether we *learn* from them.

Rainey says that in this age of speed and intensity, every marriage and family must guard against "Road Warrior Syndrome" or RWS. He adds that like any "disease," a little prevention goes a long way in stopping this terminal infection.[7]

All great leaders have strong egos. This comes out in our boldness, sense of assurance, willingness to call hard shots, and aggressiveness. All are part of what we do. If we are not willing to take risks, make decisions, and push the envelope, we aren't leading.

What can you do to keep your ego in check so that you are not blind to the dangers around the corner? Accountability to people who like you and are willing to tell you the real truth is a big part of the answer. What should your accountability look like? In his book, *Pressing On! Why Leaders Derail and What to Do about It*, Benjamin M. Kaufman gives six accountability measures.

- **Office hours:** Leaders who have specified office hours have built in a certain amount of accountability. By office hours, it is not intended to mean that a leader must be in his office eight hours a day, only that the leader keeps a schedule that others are aware of so that they can reach him.

- **Board and departmental meetings:** Some leaders would ask, "Doesn't everyone have board and departmental meetings?" The answer is no. One associate recalled that his senior pastor had a meeting with his board and staff one time per year. Another associate stated that his senior pastor had no staff meetings in the five years the associate worked with him.

- **Keeping in touch:** Do others know how to reach the leader? Some leaders purposely isolate themselves. I'm not talking about the leader who needs an occasional break and turns off his cell phone just to have a moment of rest. I'm thinking of the leader who prefers an unhealthy isolation. Others never know how or when to get in touch with him.

- **Assessments**: Deliberate assessments are valuable tools for determining one's own progress.

- **Goal setting and review:** The leader who writes out his goals at the beginning of each year and reviews or has them reviewed by others at the end of the year has instituted a system of accountability.

- **Accountability groups:** These consist of a small number of leaders who meet periodically to encourage and challenge one another.

The Bible tells us to not go it alone. ". . . not forsaking the assembling of ourselves *together*, as the manner of some is; but *exhorting* one another" (Heb. 10:25).

Notice the words "together" and "exhorting." We are in this "together" with the TEAM and with those we are accountable to.

We need to be exhorted and advised. Exhorted means someone is right alongside of a person, urging him, begging him, and strongly encouraging him to make some kind of correct decision.

In the ancient Greek world, military leaders often used this word before they sent their troops into battle. Rather than hide from the painful reality of war, the leaders would summon their troops together and speak straightforwardly with them about the potential dangers of the battlefield. The leaders would also tell their troops about the glories of winning a major victory.

Rather than ignore the clear-cut dangers of battle, these officers came right alongside their troops and urged, exhorted, beseeched, begged, and pleaded with them to stand tall; throw their shoulders back; look the enemy straight on, eyeball to eyeball; and face their battles bravely.[8]

Who do you have that tells you to face your battles bravely, fight on, and stand tall? Is your ego or past accomplishments keeping you from listening to others? Accountability is your friend. You were not created to go it alone. You can obtain great insurance from the hurricane of making a devastating decision by listening to others. So keep your ego in check and find a group of guys that like you but are willing to shoot straight with you.

Endnotes

1. Oren Harari, "Colin Powell's Seven Laws of Power," *Modern Maturity*, volume 45r, number 1 (January/February 2002): p. 48–50.

2. Del Jones, "What Do These 3 Photos Have in Common?" *USA Today* (December 10, 2003): p. 2B

3. While discussing power, failure, and accountability with a congressman, this statement was made about a common challenge political leaders face.

4. "Buying Silence: Workers Say that Tyco Perks Included Strings," The Associated Press, *Winston-Salem Journal,* January 10, 2004, p. A12.

5. John Maxwell, *Leadership: Promises for Every Day* (Nashville, TN: J. Countryman, 2003), p. 128.

6. Ted Engstrom, *The Fine Art of Mentoring* (Brentwood, TN:Wolgemuth & Hyatt, 1989), p. 34.

7. Dennis Rainey, "Staying Close on the Road," *The Life@Work Journal,* volume 3, number 5 (September/October 2000): p. 12.

8. Rick Renner, *Sparkling Gems from the Greek* (Tulsa, OK: Teach all Nations, 2003), p. 26.

CONSCIENCE — COMPROMISE

10

A conscience is a fence. There is a difference between a bad, ineffective conscience and an impulsive, stupid decision. Prince Harry decided to wear a Nazi swastika armband to his friend's birthday party as part of his costume. It was an impulsive, stupid decision; however, it was not a conscious compromise decision. He said to the media, "It was a poor choice of costume, and I apologize." His insensitivity and offensive decision, as well as his visibility, his plan to enter the Royal Military Academy, and where he would like to be one day only serve to magnify his inappropriate decision.

The newly signed pitcher of the New York Yankees, Randy Johnson, impulsively and rudely put his hand over the camera lens of the paparazzi when arriving in New York. The act was interpreted by the New York media as insensitivity to the new culture he was now a part of. Quick, impulsive, bad decision — not a conscience issue. Just tired of the stress of the media and especially the New York style of media. He, too, apologized to the public, even making sure that David Letterman knew he was sincere when appearing on the "Late Night Show."

In 1987, Gary Hart's momentum to run for president ended when he decided to spend two days with an aspiring actress named Donna Rice on a yacht named *Monkey Business.* The *National Enquirer* caught the senator in a photo with Rice on his lap with her arm around his neck. His choice derailed his dream to be the next president. Impulsive decision? Probably not. Ineffective conscience? Probably was not working too well at that time.

January 1990 marked the beginning of the end of Marion Barry's political life. As part of a sting operation jointly conducted by the FBI and the Washington police, a longtime woman friend, a "stunning former model" named Rasheeda Moore, lured Barry to a downtown hotel. [1] When Moore agreed to cooperate, the rest was easy. The mayor of Washington was videotaped buying and smoking crack cocaine, arrested on the spot, and arraigned the next day. In *How Bad Leadership Happens*, Barbara Kellerman writes, "As mayor of Washington, D.C., Marion Barry Jr. was at the far end of the spectrum. He was not a little bit intemperate; he was over the top. He was unable to manage his hungers, nor to keep them confined to his private life. Moreover, his use of drugs was, in addition to being personally and politically destructive, illegal."[2]

Prince Harry, Randy Johnson, Jimmy Baker, Kenneth Lay, Gary Hart, and Marion Barry all compromised at some level of their conscience. But there is a difference between violating our conscience with impulsive inappropriate verbiage or a decision to not be sensitive to people and that of becoming involved in an affair, breaking the law, embezzlement, and covering up wrong behavior. Prince Harry was immature and has little "memory history" of the incredible pain the Jewish people have suffered because of past or present Nazi terrorism. Jimmy Baker was largely driven by a desire for more money. Marion Barry suffered from drug addiction and a history of moral compromise.

The decision to break the law, have an affair, take advantage of the customer's vulnerability, cook the books, or do the wrong thing, are conscience issues. Freud described this as the super ego — the battle between the human conscience and selfish drives and impulses.

> ❧ SUCCESSFUL LEADERS HAVE SUCCESSFUL HABITS. THEY SACRIFICE TODAY'S PLEASURES FOR TOMORROW'S REWARDS.[3]

Character — Conscience

The conscience is a fence, a governor, within us that says, "This far and no further." It puts boundaries around us, protects us and others, and will serve us well when it is healthy and it is obeyed.

Somewhere embedded in your character is your conscience. To know a person's character is to know the governor which guides their conscience. On the steps of the Lincoln Memorial, Martin Luther King Jr. described his dream, in which his children would "one day live in a nation where thy will be judged not by the color of their skin but by the content of their character."[4]

All leaders have watched others make very bad decisions or walk away from great dreams for a moment of pleasure. We have seen friends, acquaintances, and heroes pay the price of their career, marriage, or reputation for something they "knew" was wrong. We have all been shocked by the news of another great athlete, politician, minister, or CEO that has gone over the line.

> There is a way that seems right to a man, but its end is the way to death (Prov. 16:25; ESV).

We have all wondered why, and have thought, *Could I make this same decision? What can I do to insure that I don't do this?*

It's more complicated than one might think.

Men who make bad decisions usually have several factors going on. They are involved with people. They could be tired; there might be financial pressures or just a lust for more. I agree with Barbara Kellerman, "It's impossible to teach about, learn about, leadership without teaching about, learning about, followership. And it is impossible to teach or to learn about either leadership or followership without teaching and learning about the context in which both are necessarily embedded."[5] There is the leader, the follower/s and the specifics of the situation in which their stories unfold.

The time in your life, the vulnerability you might feel when exhausted, the temptation that you're dealing with, and the personal needs you perceive that you have, all play a part in your decisions. Marriage problems, financial difficulties, emotional weakness, greed, the pressure to achieve, and the fear of failure are all contributors to what we say and do. Don't let your character get lost in the confusion of what you do.

If you are struggling with addictions, yielding to wrong temptations, or are out of control with anger, spending, or wrong behavior, you need to get help . . . now. If you don't get the help you need today, you will make choices you will regret tomorrow. The cost is too high not to deal with the personal issues that you are struggling with. Behind most of the people and behaviors discussed in this book are struggles, burnout, or extremes that should have been dealt with. The thought that *I can do one more thing, go a little further and risk a little more* is the common denominator with all who think they can get away with "whatever."

Conscience compromise affects the whole.

Kellerman writes that the decisions of the Enron hierarchy — chairman Kenneth Lay, CEO Jeffery Skilling, and CFO Andrew Fastow — "affected the lives and pocketbooks of tens of thousands of Americans, many of whom were not Enron employees. Let's be clear here. These men were not just a few rotten apples. Rather, they created, indeed encouraged, an organizational culture that allowed many apples to spoil and, in turn, ruin others."[6]

Boston's Cardinal Bernard Law (along with others in the Roman Catholic hierarchy) considered it his main mission to protect the good standing of the church. The problem was that that mission took precedence over the more immediate and humane one: to shield parishioners from predatory priests. Finally, the wrongdoing that kept the clergy's misconduct hidden from public view — the transfers, the payments, and the cover-ups — undermined the very church that the Cardinal wanted so badly to secure.[7]

> ❧ EMPTY POCKETS NEVER HELD ANYONE BACK. ONLY EMPTY HEADS AND EMPTY HEARTS CAN DO THAT.
>
> NORMAN VINCENT PEALE[8]

When leaders make decisions to do the wrong thing, it affects people all around them. Their marriages suffer greatly. Their children suffer in ways that could injure them for life. Their employees suffer and many have lost their careers because of an illegal or intemperate decision at the top. The church suffers greatly when a pastor or priest does something immoral, illegal, or unethical. Everyone pays when the leader violates his conscience or, worse yet, has no conscience. A healthy conscience helps us make right decisions.

Our conscience tells us about conflict of interest.

In her research, Barbara Kellerman found, "For those of us with an interest in leadership of any kind, the important readings in political theory are a treasure trove. They remind us — as if we need reminding — that leaders lead and followers follow not out of the kindness of their collective hearts but because it is in their self interest."[9]

THE GOOD OF THE WHOLE — OR FOR MY GOOD?

Many leaders might say they followed their conscience — however, what made their conscience tick? H.C. Trunbull said, "Conscience is not given to a man to instruct him in the right, but to prompt him to choose the right instead of the wrong when he has been instructed as to what is right. It tells a man that he ought to do right, but it does not tell him what is right. And if a man has made up his mind that a certain wrong course is the right one, the more he follows his conscience the more helpless he is as a wrongdoer."[10]

Our conscience informs us of the impulses that we struggle with.

In their book *Leadership on the Line*, Ronald Heifetz and Marty Linsky cautioned leaders to control their impulses: "We all have hungers that are expressions of our normal human needs. But sometimes those hungers disrupt our capacity to act wisely or purposefully."[11] Billy Graham said, "God put within each one of us something that cries loud against us whenever we do that which we know to be wrong. Conscience is the detective that watches the direction of our steps and decries every conscious transgression. Conscience is a vigilant eye before which each imagination, thought, and act is held up for either censure or approval. I believe there is no greater argument for the existence of God in the world today than conscience. There is no greater proof of the existence of a moral law and lawgiver in the universe than this little light of the soul. It is God's voice to the inner man. Conscience is our wisest counselor and teacher, our most faithful and most patient friend."[12]

HOW TO PROTECT GOOD LEADERSHIP AND AVOID BAD LEADERSHIP

Although there are many different types of occupations, positions, ministry paths, and political levels which require different tenures, Barbara Kellerman lists several helpful guidelines that can protect leaders.

For leaders

- Limit your tenure. When leaders remain in positions of power for too long, they acquire bad habits.
- Share power. When power is centralized, it's likely to be misused — or abused.

- Get real. Stay real. Virtually every bad leader is, to a degree, out of touch with reality.

- Compensate for your weaknesses. Leaders should surround themselves with those who know most about what they know best.

- Stay balanced. Leaders who have a healthy personal life are more likely than their workaholic counterparts to have a healthy professional life.

- Be reflective. Virtually every one of the great writers on leadership emphasizes the importance of self-knowledge, self-control, and good habits.

For followers

- Empower yourself. People who think themselves followers don't think themselves powerful. But they — we — are. Or, more accurately, they, we, can be.

- Be loyal to the whole and not to any single individual. When followers put the interests of the leader ahead of the interests of the group, the group's in trouble.

- Be skeptical. Leaders are not gods. They should be awarded no more, and no less, than the loyalty they earn.

- Be a watchdog. Ignorance is not bliss.

- Take a stand. Pliant boards, craven aids, scared subordinates, submissive underlings, and passive bystanders are as much to blame for bad leadership as are bad leaders.

- Find allies. In numbers there is strength.[13]

OUR HEALTHY CONSCIENCE CAN BE RELIED ON

"LET YOUR CONSCIENCE BE YOUR GUIDE." We have all heard and said this, countless times. Charles Swindoll said, "Conscience is like a compass. If a compass if faulty, you'll quickly get off course. A conscience gets its signals from the heart, which can be dulled, hardened, calloused. Furthermore, a conscience can be overly sensitive or can even drive one mad."

Someone who has been reared by legalistic parents who used guilt and shame to manipulate their children often has a conscience that is overly sensitive. Some have consciences so twisted and confused, they need extensive help before they can start thinking correctly. Sometimes it takes the help of a good Christian therapist — someone who can help them with a shame-based conscience — to understand how things got all fouled up. Sometimes a long-term friendship helps give grace to a conscience that has known only legalism. A conscience that is legalistic is not a good guide, nor is a libertine conscience or a calloused conscience.

In order for one's conscience to be a good guide, one the Spirit can direct, it needs to be healthy, sensitive, and capable of getting God's message and truth.[14]

Your personal faith is integrated into your leadership — your organization and its people will enjoy the "right decisions" you make. The imprints of your Christian faith on your right decisions will include the following characteristics:

- **Intentionality.** Leadership requires intentional action, and faith compels action toward spiritual integrity and ethical consistency.

- **Reflection.** This discipline leads to spiritual depth, greater self-knowledge, and organizational insight.

- **Self-evaluation.** Submit to the mirror test. Ask, "Is the person I see the person I say I am and want to be?" Leading from faith is the willingness to receive feedback and to correct course when necessary.

- **Sense of vocation.** Leadership carries with it a sense of calling for the faithful.

- **Professional expertise.** Leadership is not something one can fake; it requires adequate preparation and excellence in the field.

- **Covenant building.** Faithful leaders build alliances, create communities, seek partnerships, and promote teaming.

- **Service.** Leaders of faith seek to serve their organizations while subordinating their egos and asking what needs to be done (rather than thinking about what they want to do).

- **Intellectual integrity.** To borrow Peter Drucker's phrase, intellectual integrity is the ability to see the world as it is, not as we want it to be. This is a discipline of faith, and it is the ability to live in reality. Leaders with intellectual integrity never stop increasing their knowledge about human nature and the world.[15]

The responsibility you have to those around you is bigger than you. Sensitivity to your healthy conscience is necessary for every leader. Greatness goes away when we violate our sense of "rightness." Conscience sensitivity is doable — you do not have to cross the line.

CONSCIENCE — COMPROMISE

DECIDE TO DO THE RIGHT THING — REGARDLESS

The first mention of sin in the Bible is when Adam and Eve yielded to temptation. They were tempted to do something that God told them not to do. The word "sin" is also used as an archer's term. When the arrow misses the bulls-eye it is called sin; it missed the mark. Human decisions that disobey the Word of God are called sin because they miss the heart of the target — doing the right thing — being obedient to truth and being sensitive to our God-given conscience. Both Adam and Eve were tempted to do what God told them not to do; both knew better, both decided to disobey God and their conscience, and both paid an incredible price. The Bible tells us that they knew the rules: "You may surely eat of every tree of the garden, but of the tree of the knowledge of good and evil you shall not eat, for in the day that you eat of it you shall surely die" (Gen. 2:16–17; ESV). They made a conscious decision, and they paid the price of not doing the right thing.

When we disobey our conscience, we know what we are doing. We are choosing to play Russian roulette. The gamble has begun. Will we get away with it — or not? Will this decision kill me, or will I just hear the click of the hammer? Obeying your conscience is choosing not to gamble with the wrong decision. When we choose to cross the line of right and wrong, to heal or to hurt, to be honest or dishonest, to sleep with her or not; we have gone too far.

To gamble with the "rightness and wrongness" of something is too big of a gamble. Most of the time, the choice to do the right thing is clear — when it looks muddy, take time to think and evaluate it. Your conscience will come to a clear decision. We all remember the day of the *Challenger* tragedy. It was found that the O-ring was defective. If the O-ring was in any way leaking, cracked, or imperfect, the space shuttle didn't go up. However, in the investigation that followed the event it was discovered that the team members knew of the possibility that the rings might fail, but they told no one. The choice not to speak up was a terrible decision. We don't question the motives of those who knew of the possible malfunction; we do wonder why they decided just to let the launch go as planned.

The right decision is our choice — so is the wrong decision.

In *The End of Management and the Rise of Organizational Democracy*, Kenneth Cloke and Joan Goldsmith give a helpful list of how to connect our values with our decisions.

- Significance: What values are at play in this decision?
- Universalizability: What would happen if everyone did what I am about to do?

- Leadership: What would happen if no one did what I am about to do?
- Reciprocity: How would I feel if the same standard were applied to me?
- Publicity: How would I feel if my action was made public?
- Defensibility: How easy would it be to justify the action to others?
- Responsibility: Am I willing to take responsibility for the action or inaction, no matter what the outcome?
- Intuition: Does the action feel right or wrong to me?
- Legacy: Am I willing for my children to live with the consequences of my action or inaction?[16]

When we ask ourselves these kinds of questions, the muddy water clears up and we can sense our conscience or the temptation to compromise.

There are too many books, seminars, and conferences on becoming great leaders and building our organization or church to a point of tremendous success. We need to occasionally take a look at the price people have paid when they made the choice to do the wrong thing.

❧ **WHEN WE CONSIDER THE COST OF NOT DOING THE RIGHT THING — IT'S NOT WORTH IT.**

The careers that were lost, the financial ruin they have experienced, the marriages that were destroyed, and the effect on their children, peers, employees, and friends, because they did not fight the temptation to act inappropriately or illegally. Looking at and thinking about what others have experienced because of not being sensitive to a healthy conscience can help us be disciplined in our decisions and actions.

> No temptation has overtaken us that is not common to man. God is faithful, and he will not let you be tempted beyond your ability, but with the temptation he will also provide the way of escape, that you may be able to endure it (1 Cor. 10:13; ESV).

Endnotes

1. T. Morgenthau and M. Miller, "Busting the Mayor," *Newsweek* (January 29, 1990): p. 24. This article provides a description of the episode.
2. Barbara Kellerman, *Bad Leadership: What It Is, How It Happens, Why It Matters* (Boston, MA: Harvard Business School Press, 2004) p. 115.
3. Lee J. Colan, *Minds & Hearts* (Dallas, TX: CornerStone Leadership Institute), p. 55.

CONSCIENCE — COMPROMISE

4. Dr. Martin Luther King Jr., "I Have a Dream" speech, August 28, 1963, Washington, DC.

5. Barbara Kellerman, "How Bad Leadership Happens," *Leader to Leader*, number 35 (Winter 2005): p 45.

6. Kellerman, *Bad Leadership: What It Is, How It Happens, Why It Matters*, p. 11.

7. For the full accounting of the crisis in the Boston diocese, see: Investigative Staff of the *Boston Globe, Betrayal: The Crisis in the Catholic Church* (Boston, MA: Little, Brown and Co., 2002).

8. Colan, *Minds & Hearts*, p. 57.

9. Kellerman, "How Bad Leadership Happens," p. 42.

10. Charles Swindoll, *The Tale of the Tardy Oxcart* (Nashville, TN: Word Pub., 1998), p. 118.

11. Ronald A Heifetz and Marty Linsky, *Leadership on the Line: Staying Alive through the Dangers of Leading* (Boston, MA: Harvard Business School Press, 2002), p. 164.

12. Quoted in George Sweeting, *Great Quotes and Illustrations* (Waco, TX: Word Books, 1985), p. 60.

13. Kellerman, "How Bad Leadership Happens," p. 45.

14. Swindoll, *The Tale of The Tardy Oxcart*, p. 117.

15. Bernice Ledbetter, www.right.com, quoted in *Life@Work*, volume 3, number 6 (November/December 2000): p. 16.

16. Dave Ulrich, Steve Kerr, and Ron Ashkenas, "General Electric's Leadership 'Work-Out,' " *Leader to Leader*, number 35 (Winter 2005): p. 51.

11

MENTORS AND COACHES

Many have fallen because of being influenced by people who set a bad example. We don't need to remind ourselves of the young men who have been affected by the failure of their father or older brother, the churches that have been damaged by the compromise of a pastor or priest, or the company that has been severely injured by the mismanagement of the CEO. It's all around us, it's devastating, and it ought to motivate us to seek out worthy examples, that is, people who lived years ago or people alive now who can serve as examples of what we want to become.

The 12 disciples that became apostles in the New Testament had Jesus. Young Timothy had Paul. Joshua led a tremendous nation and won battle after battle, but he had Moses as an example to show him how to lead. Elisha performed more miracles than his "coach" Elijah. However, Elijah was his example of keeping focused, being brave, believing God, and doing the right thing. Positive examples are tremendous motivators for success. Negative examples are tremendous motivators for (and excuses for) failure.

Jimmy Bakker grew up in poverty in Muskegon, Michigan, and was "embarrassed about [his] family house." He says, "Whenever someone drove me home from school, I'd ask to be dropped off several blocks away so they wouldn't see the house."[1] As a child who grew up in church, Jimmy was embarrassed that his pastor painted Sunday school classrooms purple simply because the paint was free.

Bakker had to repeat his senior year in high school because of poor grades, and though he often said that he was a graduate of North Central Bible College, he didn't graduate. He was small in physical stature when in college — weighing about 130 pounds. His mother was cold and self-involved while his father was stern, judgmental, hardworking, and tight with what little money the family had.[2]

His life was filled with the kind of examples that encourage tremendous insecurity. Feeling inferior to other people because of his background, education, and poverty was very likely a major driving force in his achievements; however, this was also a motivator for his failure. There is no excuse for his misuse of funds, his affair, or the deception he engaged in. However, looking at the examples in his life can give us some understanding about *why* he made some of his tragic decisions.

> Whoever walks with the wise becomes wise, but the companion of fools will suffer harm (Prov. 13:20; ESV).

Not all of us have had a father, friend, coach, or mentor in our life that we want to follow. But we can still learn how to be a growing leader by learning from other great leaders. We can read about, seek out, and find people who will coach us to greatness in our chosen field.

THE POWER OF AN EXAMPLE

You have largely become what you have observed and respected. You've heard,

> ❧ SOMEWHERE EARLY ON OUR WAY, WE EAT ONE OF THE WONDERFUL FRUITS OF THE TREE OF KNOWLEDGE, THINGS SEPARATE INTO GOOD AND EVIL, AND WE BEGIN THE SHADOW-MAKING PROCESS; WE DIVIDE OUR LIVES.[3]

"Children learn by what they see, not by what they hear." I think that is true with adults, too. When leaders demand punctuality but are always late — followers do likewise. When the boss takes advantage of the company — so do employees. The culture of your organization or church is established from the top down. The influence of a good example is tremendous. If we want to work with good followers, we have to set the example by being good leaders.

Albert Bandura, professor of psychology at Stanford University, said, "Modeling is the first step in developing competencies." In his book *Self-Efficacy: The Exercise of Control*, he wrote, "We had this reinforced for us when we did some research on the leader-as-coach. In that study we found that of all the items used to measure coaching behavior, the one most linked to success is "this person embodies character qualities and values that I admire."[4]

EXAMPLE LESSONS WE MUST LEARN

Example #1 — Leaders view difficulties as their friends and challenges as opportunities to grow.

It is often said that "what gets rewarded gets done." I don't believe this is the reason good leaders become great leaders. I believe that people become great because of passion for what they do, conviction that comes from the heart, and courage that drives through fear. This is a large part of the driving force that cuts through mediocrity. Money, perks, or location isn't the motivator for greatness. Passion, conviction, and heart-felt determination push leaders to a higher level of accomplishment. There is no correlation between courage of convictions and pay for performance.

All leaders have tremendous challenges and all potential leaders must learn that that challenge is their friend. Leaders have learned to see value in the crisis and in the situation that looks impossible. In E.L. Deci's book, *Why We Do What We Do*, Deci points out that there has to be something significant in the challenge itself that makes the struggle worthwhile. When it comes to excellence, it's definitely not "what gets rewarded gets done," but rather "what is rewarding gets done."

Most of the time we have learned to handle tough times because of the way a significant other, like a father, boss, mentor, teacher, or coach has handled it. I remember a coach that I had for one season in track and field. I also remember a missionary, and another great leader who served in Calcutta, India. Along the journey of life, I have had people that I watched from a distance, and some that gave their time to coach me, to guide me, and had the courage to tell me when I needed to adjust. Watching them handle tough times and seemingly impossible situations has taught me valuable lessons.

In her book *Jesus, CEO*, Laurie Beth Jones wrote about a CEO of an osteopathic hospital that she has worked with. "After a meeting in which some new directions for the hospital were presented, several of the mid-level managers grew concerned about the potential upset it might have to those who were used to doing things as before. This leader calmly listened to their fears (for the 14th time) and then turned to the person in charge of implementing the changes and said simply, 'Proceed as planned.' The simple directive indicated that, as captain, he had set his sights on the goal and wasn't about to be drawn off course by factionary arguments among the crew. He was acting on his aerial view." She adds, "When I look at people occupying powerful seats in Congress and the presidency itself, I do not forget the many attacks, vilifications, insults, and opposition they endured in order to attain their powerful status. Influence doesn't come easily."[5]

Difficulties, challenges, and seemingly impossible situations can be your greatest friend. They force you to look deeper, explore possibilities, pray, and dream of other ways that you might have ignored.

Example #2 — Leaders are mentally tough but heart sensitive.

Stress doesn't make us discouraged or ill — how we respond to stressful events in our lives does. The attitudinal differences between high-stress/high-illness people and high-stress/low-illness people are significant. The way the high-stress/low-illness leaders handle stress promotes success and it seems to push them to the next level or at least to have greater focus on the task at hand.

Leaders can't lead if they are not psychologically tough. Those in our company or organization will not follow us if we avoid stressful events and vacillate on taking action. To accept the challenge of change and the normalcy of a crisis in life, we need to believe that we can overcome adversity. Many leaders let stress get to them, or manage the stressful situation in the way they have seen another leader handle it. Psychological toughness while remaining tender in our heats is something that we grow in.

Laurie Jones tells a story of the captain of an aircraft carrier in the South China Sea. "Your crewman suddenly alerts you that a plane is approaching. The message says that it is South Vietnamese, and it is running out of fuel. The plane must land on your deck or perish in the sea. The pilot says that aboard are himself, his wife, and their five children. They are escaping from North Vietnam. There is only one small problem. There is no room on the deck for them and no time to move the other planes. What would you do? The captain pushed three multimillion-dollar aircraft into the sea."[6]

Being mentally tough, clear thinking, and having a sensitive heart is all part of being the leader we want to be. Who are you watching and who is in your life as a coach to assist you in your desire to grow in this area?

Example # 3 — Greatness demonstrates and expects trust.

You can't do it alone. Leadership is not a solo act; it's a team performance. Challenges require more collaboration, not less. James Kouzes said, "The increasing emphasis on networks, business-to-business and peer-to-peer e-commerce, strategic acquisitions, and knowledge work, along with the surging number of global alliances and local partnerships, is testimony to the fact that in a more complex, wired world, the winning strategies will be based on 'we, not I' philosophy. Collaboration is a social imperative. Without it, people can't get extraordinary things done in organizations."[7]

You simply cannot lead if those you lead don't trust you — or if you don't trust them. Without trust on both sides of the fence you cannot get the extraordinary thing done. The challenge will prove to be too much and the crisis will seem insurmountable. Leaders who stay out front create a sense of trust, based on mutual respect and caring. Talent does not intimidate them; in fact, they trust so much that they hire strong people to serve with them and will trust them to lead. When I have hired people to work on my team, I follow this rule. Humble, hard working, talented, and smart. I hire "spirit" before I hire experience. When they come on board, I begin to trust them and demonstrate to them that they can trust me.

> Without counsel plans fail, but with many advisers they succeed (Proverbs 15:22; ESV).

If trust is something we struggle with — then leadership at a higher level will likely be out of reach. The untrustworthy leader always questions the advice, intuitions, and work ethic of those around him, and the team will mirror this attitude back to him. The leader's lack of trust in others will result in the other's lack of trust in him.

In her book *Jesus, CEO*, Laurie Beth Jones wrote about a discussion she had with a man from another country who was envious of American people's ability to form teams in America. "When your people want to get something done, they gather a group and assign the tasks. In my country, unfortunately, we do not have it so easy. Many of us cannot even seem to sit down together at the table. We spend years playing King of the Mountain, while your people have already figured out how to move it, save it, or make it bigger." She said,

MENTORS AND COACHES

> **❧ TRUSTING THE TEAM AND DEMONSTRATING TO THEM HOW THEY CAN TRUST YOU IS KEY TO ANY LEADER'S SUCCESS.**

"One of the most important keys to successful teamwork is agreeing to agree. If you as a leader or manager intend to accomplish anything significant, the first step toward attaining your goal is to create a team. Yet many people still feel they must do everything alone. We still have John Wayne's and Super Moms who think it is wrong or a sign of weakness to ask for help."[8]

Example # 4 — Leaders know how to create healthy relationships.

Daniel Goleman has made many aware of emotional intelligence (EI), which is described this way. "Emotional Intelligence — the ability to manage ourselves and our relationships effectively — consists of four fundamental capabilities: Self-awareness, self-management, social awareness, and social skill."[9]

Relationships are critical for those who are leaders. In fact, everyone should be greatly concerned about relationships because that is the way we're wired. All of us are relational, all of us are emotional, and all of us want healthy relationships. Every day in the newspaper or on the evening news, we see examples of unhealthy relationships. The abuse scandal of the Roman Catholic Church has cost various dioceses millions of dollars. The unhealthy relationships between priest/pastor and the children or adults in his care has not only cost this church money, but has caused great injury to the lives of those who have been taken advantage of. The scandals with CEOs, CFOs, and upper management have caused insurmountable damage to their whole companies. They caused great injury to the organizations, and also, the countless people who have been emotionally and relationally injured for who knows how long.

Leadership needs to be a healthy relationship between those who are leaders and those who follow. Relationships can be between two people or many. Leadership is relationship. Becoming socially competent is part of the package of developing as a leader. Honest confrontation, instruction, or coaching cannot happen if we do not have a relationship with those we lead. We can go to the finest universities, seminaries, or conferences. We can read the best information about leadership, and we can observe the greatest leaders in our career field; however, without relational skills (social skills) the likelihood of failure versus success, is high. A class on "people skills" should be required in every major that is offered in our universities and seminaries. In fact, everyone should be required to get an A+ in the class if they want to be a leader!

People skills, communication skills, and healthy relationship skills are key to the balanced package of keeping us on the "integrity tracks" of life. There are many examples of executives who have demonstrated sensitivity to people and seem to know the right things to say at the right time. Watch them, learn from them, and let them become part of the way you do things.

Example # 5 — Choosing to lead in *the right way*, is the right choice.

"You name it and we've done it." Ideas come and go, but "I've observed one constant theme across all of them — leaders have to step forward and get involved with change. Although each idea on how to do change is somewhat different — and they all have some good parts — without leadership, nothing works " said Vince Russo, executive director of the Aeronautical Systems Center at Wright-Patterson Air Force Base.[10]

The opportunity to become a leader or to grow as a leader comes throughout our lives. It is not a passing fad; it is a gift and it's critically important to you as you accomplish all that you were created to do. In these uncertain times globally, your decision to lead with integrity is critical. Leadership matters more in times of uncertainty. Difficult days and crisis events are opportunities for the leader to step to the plate and do the right thing. Someone must make the decision, call the shot, and do what needs to be done. A crisis demands courage. Doing the right thing isn't always the popular thing; however, great leaders do it anyway. All of us have chances to make decisions that will affect companies, churches, and cities that are in a crisis. Many of us have had good and bad examples in our lives. Choosing to remember the good ones and avoid the bad ones is our call.

> Remember your leaders, who spoke the word of God to you. Consider the outcome of their way of life and imitate their faith (Heb. 13:7; NIV).

Their message is worth remembering
Their life is worth living
Their faith is worth imitating

If today's churches, companies, and organizations want to be thriving tomorrow, they have an obligation to coach and mentor the new generation of leaders.

Challenges in life always need leaders and leaders seek challenges. Bad stuff happens in good organizations even when good leaders are in place. Great leaders must handle these challenges and crises with integrity and psychological

Mentors and Coaches

hardness. Finding mentors, fathers, and coaches to help us do what we do is part of being the leader we want to be. All of us have to be "lifelong learners." Leaders are readers, disciples want to be taught, and everyone has gifts within that need to be coached to excellence.

LOOKING FOR A COACH?

Mentors, coaches, and great examples in our lives are critical. Today's leaders have the responsibility to equip and empower the next generation of leaders. Researchers asked nearly 6,000 executives from 77 large companies, "What contributed most to your professional development over the course of your career?" It was discovered that there were 16 things that gave them the focus they needed. Following is the percentage of executives who considered each strategy "absolutely essential" or "very important" to their professional and personal development.

The way jobs are structured	81%
Informal coaching/feedback	**73%**
Role models	**71%**
Told weaknesses/strengths	**71%**
Speed of job rotation/advancement	63%
Special project assignments	61%
Being mentored	**60%**
360° feedback	**54%**
Job rotation across areas	50%
Development plans	46%
Formal performance evaluation	**43%**
Traditional training within the company	36%
Individual learning	33%
Other nontraditional learning programs	32%
Traditional training outside the company	30%
Testing/assessment by outside agency	10%[11]

The areas I have put in bold all have to do with coaching and mentoring. Disciples are learners. Coaches and mentors are examples to those they have influence over. All of us need people who have a good influence on who we are becoming. Every leader needs to reflect on the kind of influence he is to those he leads. A job coach or life coach is a great idea. Before allowing a coach to give direction to your life:

- Tell your prospective coach why you think he might be a good coach for you.
- Let him know that you want to learn from his failures as well as his successes in life.
- Ask if he might be willing to spend a certain number of hours with you a month.
- Let him know that you will cover the expenses, for example, phone calls, travel, meals, as well as what both of you feel is a reasonable cost for the time.
- Reassure the prospective coach that you do not expect him to secure a promotion for you.
- Remind him again and again that you want to develop professionally and personally.
- Inform him about how you envision he might be able to assist you — serve as a sounding board, give perspective, teach life lessons, etc.
- Be clear that you see an end to the coaching relationship and are not expecting lifelong friendship (keep the commitment to six months or a year).
- Give the coach a way out. In other words, say that he can stop coaching you at any time for any reason — without hurt feelings.

> ❧ THE FRIEND IN MY ADVERSITY I SHALL ALWAYS CHERISH MOST. I CAN BETTER TRUST THOSE WHO HELPED TO RELIEVE THE GLOOM OF MY DARK HOURS THAN THOSE WHO ARE SO READY TO ENJOY WITH ME THE SUNSHINE OF MY PROSPERITY.
> — ULYSSES S. GRANT

Endnotes

1. Charles E. Shepard, *Forgiven: The Rise and Fall of Jim Bakker and the PTL Ministry* (New York: Atlantic Monthly Press, 1989), p. 546.
2. Ibid., p. 556.

MENTORS AND COACHES

3. Robert A. Johnson, *Owning Your Own Shadow: Understanding the Dark Side of the Psyche* (San Francisco, CA: Harper San Francisco, 1991), p. 4.

4. James M. Kouzes and Barry Z. Pozner, "Challenge Is the Opportunity for Greatness," *Leader to Leader* (Spring 2003): p. 17.

5. Laurie Beth Jones, *Jesus, CEO* (New York: Hyperion, 1994), p. 160–161.

6. Ibid., p. 248.

7. *Leader to Leader* (Spring 2003): p. 21.

8. Jones, *Jesus, CEO*, p. 91.

9. Kouzes and Pozner, "Challenge Is the Opportunity for Greatness," p. 22.

10. Ibid., p. 23.

11. Helen Handfield-Jones, "Grow Great Executives: Give Them Great Jobs," *Leader to Leader*, number 14 (Fall 1999): p. 12.

12
twelve

ETHICS

W hen we watch a great leader fall, our "emotional wind" is taken away. We wonder, "Why?" "Is there anyone else involved?" "How long has this been going on?"

For sure, this can be discouraging. We had hoped for more from certain people. We also want to protect ourselves from the same kind of compromise. People who are "clean," who verbalize integrity, and live normal lives are who we want as leaders. However, when people *look* clean, *seem* to say all the right things, and are careful to cover their "legal" bases concerning how they live, while compromising morally, ethically, and legally behind the scenes, it causes shock and the fall-out affects the entire organization. Why? Because we expected more, we wanted more, we simply believed that our leader was at least attempting to be ethical.

> Like a muddied spring or a polluted well is a righteous man who gives way to the wicked (Prov. 25:26; NIV).

The pollution in "a well" that looks pure can ruin a man and can wipe out an organization. When Warren Buffett, CEO of Berkshire Hathaway, chooses people to lead in his organization, he says, "In looking for people to hire, you look for three qualities: integrity, intelligence, and energy. If you don't have the first, the other two will kill you. Think about it; it's true. If you hire somebody without the first, you really want them to be dumb and lazy. When contemplating any business act, an employee should ask himself whether he would be willing to see it immediately described by an informed and critical reporter on the front page of his local paper, there to be read by his spouse, children, and friends . . . we simply want no part of any activities that pass legal tests, but that we, as citizens, would find offensive. . . . It takes 20 years to build a reputation, and five minutes to ruin it. If you think about that, you'll do things differently."[1]

THE ETHICAL CHALLENGE — HOW TO LEAD WITH UNYIELDING INTEGRITY

Some have gotten away with walking on the edge and shooting below the ethical radar. Possibly they picked a *modus operendi* from watching another leader get away with something similar. The Bible talks about people who lived a double standard, "Even while these people were worshiping the LORD, they were serving their idols" (2 Kings 17:41; NIV). "Worshiping the Lord — serving idols?" It doesn't mix. The water is muddy and the well is polluted.

Some leaders really don't get it

The man shouted to me: "What do ethics have to do with anything? What are ethics anyway? You have no right to make these kinds of rules!"

These comments demonstrated the "in your face" attitude of a former employee who wanted his perks and influence to continue after he left our organization. He wanted benefits, rights, power, and influence, years after he left. He refused to understand why I said, "We can't allow this." The problem was, when he worked for us, he had the same attitude. Thus, he influenced a lot of people in his department to be cynical, caustic, and calloused. He wanted power, he wanted exposure, and by golly he would do whatever he wanted, no matter who he had to walk over or misrepresent himself to.

It's all around us

Jeffrey Immelt wrote, "We've witnessed, over the last six to nine months in this country, what I would say is the equivalent of a corporate freak show. It's been a time when everything's been reversed, when all our excesses have been exposed."[2]

Why are ethics important? *INFLUENCE*

Ethics is the discipline to do the "right thing." It is a framework that is covered with sound moral principles and decisions. It is a moral grid through which our decisions in life are made — both in our personal lives and in our organizations. Ethics are critical to the morale of any business or church. How high you set the ethical bar determines, to a large extent, where your peers, employees, parishioners, and your kids will set theirs. Robert Cialdini, president of *Influence At Work* wrote, "The power of influence is so strong that leaders need to be ruthless about rooting out dishonesty and deception in the way the organization deals with its customers, clients, regulators, suppliers, employees, and vendors. Leaders who tolerate anything less will pay a heavy price, because employees tend to ascend or tumble to the level of their leaders."[3] In our universities, Greham's law is taught in economics classes. It states "Bad money drives out good money." The same works in companies, corporate offices, and churches. Unethical behavior drives out ethical behavior. In the recent corporate scandals we have witnessed, the organization as a whole was corrupt. It started at the top, or the top was unwilling to address certain issues.

Leaders must have strong ethical sensitivity. Jeffery Immelt, wrote, "The CEO today has to be the moral leader of the company — the way you talk about your company externally and the way you run it internally."[4] CEOs also need to ensure that they have people around them who have the same ethical compass. Dennis Haley, CEO of Academy Leadership, said, "Scandals were at the very least enabled by yes men and yes women who adapted, chameleon-like."[5] When leaders compromise, they want people around them who will not get in their way. The effect of leaders operating below the radar has sent a huge message to our customers, clients, and parishioners. The message is, "Question everything they say, because they speak out of both sides of their mouth, depending on who they are with and what they want."

The Pain — The Damage — The Lack of Trust

The damage this does to trust is huge and often takes years (if it's even possible) to build back. Many times, people decide *not* to trust someone, for very good reasons. The Catholic parishioner wonders if they should leave their children alone with a priest. The investor wonders if the stockbroker is trying to help him, or pad his own pocket. The customer wonders if the rebate had "small print" rules that the salesman "forgot" to tell them. Churchgoers wonder if they should listen to a message from the so-called man of God who flirts with women, or is verbally abusive to his wife. The child wonders about the dad who says one thing and does another. The wife wonders about her husband who says he will be working hard on a business trip and finds out that the agenda wasn't anything like he described.

Not only do people within our organizations begin to mistrust, but also they begin setting their moral bar lower. Robert Cialdine wrote, "Leaders who want to create and maintain healthy, ethical organizations need to be constantly vigilant. It is critically important to set standards and to recognize that even small deviations from those standards can lead to trouble. When we break an ethical barrier it is just like breaking a pane of glass: it's gone; it doesn't exist anymore. Once you've crossed that barrier your self-perception changes: things that were previously off-limits may now seem acceptable."

The "broken glass" can't be repaired to look flawless. Breaking ethical rules takes a lot of time to fix. The company (or church) that compromised their standards sent a message of caution to the customer (or parishioner) that could take years to repair. The pastor who was caught looking at pornography and the boss who tried to undermine his peers caused those around them to question the "truth" of what he says or does. Employees or top-notch volunteers who watch their boss or leader be dishonest to a supplier become uneasy about their job security. I recently heard about a situation a person found himself in. "I was talking to our president and some other people on the executive team after some difficult negotiations with a major supplier, and I wasn't comfortable with how it had gone. One of the vice presidents had lied to the supplier to get the price down. I don't remember my exact words, but I put it as diplomatically as I knew how that I wasn't comfortable with that, and that it could undermine our relationship with the supplier.

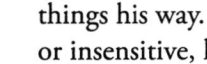

CHARACTER IS CONTAGIOUS!

"The president rolled his eyes and laughed. 'Look at Jack! He's shocked, shocked, that we sometimes tell stories to suppliers!' Everyone laughed, and someone said, 'Grow up, Jack.'

"Well, I turned red, but I remember thinking, If they are willing to lie to suppliers, why not employees? I never trusted the executive team after that."

Bad company ruins good morals (1 Cor. 15:33; RSV).

Unethical behavior can be contagious. If a leader has questionable ethics, those who are on his team will either develop similar ethical standards or leave the organization because they are not comfortable with the "stress" of doing things his way. If the boss is untruthful, bends or breaks the rules, or is dishonest or insensitive, his behavior makes that type of activity more acceptable to the other leaders. When a leader decides to get a "mail order degree" to achieve a certain status, those who are watching and working with him *think* that is the way to get ahead. Bad examples lead to bad behavior throughout the organization.

When living in Europe, my family and I attended a four-day Christian leaders' conference. This conference normally ended with a worship service on the conference grounds. When we arrived for the baptismal service, I noticed several topless ladies sitting around the pool where the event was to happen. I also saw one of the leaders' teenage sons take off his tennis shorts and underwear and bend over and put on his bathing suit — in the process "mooning" numerous people sitting around the swimming pool.

I immediately avoided the area and protected my children by going to an area where we could not see these people.

Talking to one of the leaders, I said, "It seems that if our Christian conference has totally booked this hotel, we ought to be able to prevent people who want to sunbathe in the nude from doing so in public."

He laughed at me and said, "You're new here, aren't you? You'll get used to it — like the rest of us have."

I remember commenting as I turned and walked away from the area, "I hope not."

COMPROMISE WALKS SLOWLY

There is a subtle desensitizing that can happen with standards, morals, rules of organizations, and ethics. It might not happen overnight, but over time people within organizations develop new "unwritten" rules and standards. In fact, once the clock strikes 13, many wonder if 12 is really midnight. There's not a lot of training out there.

Ethics training is a low priority in most companies and parishes. *USA Today* reported that, "Despite all of the corporate scandals, most workers received no ethics training in the last 12 months."[6] Seventy-two percent of the corporations reported that there was no ethical training, while 28 percent had training.

I recently asked a denominational district officer who was the director of over 400 churches, if there were any ethical programs or standards set for his district. He said he had no guidelines regarding ethics for his district. I asked the question because I had noticed that several of the ministers were taking liberties to stay connected with and even harassing the leadership of churches they no longer served. Many were performing weddings, funerals, and other official functions without checking with the present leadership. The activity was causing confusion and disloyalty within the congregations. This would be like a previous executive of a company coming back occasionally and performing official functions for the company without the new executives' permission or knowledge. Or like a former coach coaching from

ETHICS

the sidelines during a football game where some of his former players were still playing.

I had watched a particular minister within that district repeatedly break ethical rules and do whatever he felt would get him ahead. He criticized other ministers, tried to turn staff and parishioners against current leadership, got upset and tried to intimidate ministers who cautioned him about his behavior, and basically operated by his own set of rules. Oh, he wasn't committing adultery, stealing money from the church, or lying *in public* — but he was certainly operating over the edge with what was healthy and right. The district knew that he was doing these things; others had told leadership, but leadership was unwilling to "hassle" with it. This man's behavior strongly damaged the other pastors' ability to build trust and rapport within their churches.

WHAT ARE THE UNCOMPROMISING STANDARDS?

I understand that you might be reading this and thinking, *It's not possible not to compromise some; it's too complicated today.*

I don't think so. The Creator of you, me, and this world will help us understand "right" standards to live by. He can help us understand how we ought to operate our organization, how we should treat people, and what decisions cross the line of compromise.

Bruce Kennedy, the former CEO of Alaska Airlines, made it clear that his faith gave him the wisdom and strength to lead that airline company to profits that surprised many. "When I took over as president, we grossed a hundred million dollars a year. Ten years later we grossed one billion dollars a year. I thought, well, if ten years from now I look back and I've done more of the same, what significance would it have. I felt restless to do something for Christ. I had to make the commitment to leave what I was doing, and make myself available for Christian volunteer work."[7]

Edward Land, founder of Polaroid, had a similar commitment to the bottom line of doing the right thing. His famous quote, "The bottom line is in heaven" has characterized his leadership goals, and his life.[8]

The uncompromising standards of leaders according to James MacGregor Burns are, "Leadership occurs when one or more persons engage with others in such a way that leaders and followers raise one another to higher levels of motivation and morality."[9] Burns suggests the following ethical codes:

- Ethical leaders put their follower's needs before their own. Unethical leaders do not.

- Ethical leaders exemplify private virtues such as courage and temperance. Unethical leaders do not.

- Ethical leaders exercise leadership in the interest of the common good. Unethical leaders do not.

William Pollard, CEO of ServiceMaster, has led a billion-dollar company by believing that every human being, including custodians, lawn care personnel, and laundry workers are created in the image of God. His understanding and implementation of this has brought dignity and contentment to tens of thousands of people who work in these important occupations.[10] When evaluating your personal ethical standards and the way you operate in your organization there are three things that are paramount. Since you were created in the "image of God," everyone who works in your organization, the people you serve, those who live and work next door — all people — are created in the image of God. The one who created you wants you to act like Him. The three "godlike" characteristics that have a direct impact on your ethical decision-making are:

God is loving, therefore I need to be a loving person in all my relationships. The person who desires to be like Christ focuses on the needs of the other person without concern for his or her own prerogatives or rights. Loving people within our organizations means being sensitive to their needs, doing more than the law requires, and going the "extra mile."[11]

God is just, therefore I need to be just and fair in the way I treat people. When we work with people, there will always be times when we need to ask ourselves, "Is this right, is this fair, am I being biased in my decision?" On the other hand, many people misunderstand justice. If we have an employee who has broken all the rules, or significantly crossed the line, do we need to keep them as an employee? Forgiveness doesn't mean you have to let a person keep hurting you or your organization. When God forgives us of our sins or bad decisions, we still suffer many of the consequences of those decisions. If we have employees who have the habit of not obeying the rules, or of trying to get away with things, we can forgive them, but we need to continue to challenge them to do what is right. This doesn't mean that we necessarily trust them right away. If someone has a lying problem, you might forgive them, but you don't blindly start believing everything they say. Trust takes time. Forgiveness is immediate, but trust must be rebuilt little by little.

God is fair in the way He treats us, and as leaders we should reflect His justice.

ETHICS

God is holy, therefore I need to understand that there are right and wrong ways of doing things. Every quality organization has a personnel manual. This is a document that gives basic instructions about how to work within the organization. God has a personnel manual, too. It's called the Holy Bible. Holy means separate, doing things the right way, obeying the rules. Of course, not all organizations operate by the same set of standards. Some have high integrity, some are a little gray, and some try to get away with whatever they can. We constantly need to ask ourselves if we are doing things the right way. We must run our organization and treat people like our Creator would if He were the CEO. The late Martyn Lloyd-Jones, considered by many to be one of the greatest speakers of the 20th century, wrote the following: "As you go on living this righteous life, and practicing it with all your might and energy, and all your time . . . you will find that the process that went on before, in which you went on from bad to worse and became viler and viler, is entirely reversed. You will become cleaner and cleaner, and purer and purer, and holier and holier, and more and more conformed unto the image of the Son of God."[12]

Men's leader and author Ted Engstrom wrote:

The World Needs Men . . .

Who cannot be bought,

Whose word is their bond,

Who put character above wealth,

Who possess opinions and a will,

Who are larger than their vocations,

Who do not hesitate to take chances,

Who will not lose their individuality in a crowd,

Who will be as honest in small things as in great things,

Who will make no compromise with wrong,

Whose ambitions are not confined to their own selfish desires,

Who will not say they do it "because everybody else does it,"

Who are true to their friends through good report and evil report, in adversity as well as in prosperity,

Who do not believe that shrewdness, cunning, and hardheadedness are the best qualities for winning success,

Who are not ashamed or afraid to stand for the truth when it is unpopular,

Who say "no" with emphasis, although the rest of the world is saying "yes."[13]

Endnotes

1. Noel M. Tichy and Andrew R. McGill, *The Ethical Challenge* (San Francisco, CA: Jossey-Bass, 2003), p. 9.

2. Noel Tichy and Andrew McGill, *The Ethical Challenge* (San Francisco, CA: Jossey-Bass, 2003), p. 111.

3. Robert Cialdini, "Creating an Ethical Environment," *Leader to Leader* (Spring, 2003): p. 9.

4. Tichy and McGill, *The Ethical Challenge*, p. 112.

5. "Good Followers Speak Up When Boss Is Wrong," *USA Today* (December 10, 2003): p. 2B.

6. *USA Today* (January 29, 2004): Section 1B.

7. Robert Schuller, Hour of Power, *Abide in your Calling*, www.sermons.org/callofgod1,html.

8. www.zaadz.com/quotes/authors/EdwardherbertLamb.

9. James MacGregor Burns, *Leadership* (New York: Harper & Row, 1978), p. 18, 20.

10. Ibid., p 19.

11. Matthew 5:41 tells us, "And if someone forces you to go one mile, go with him two miles" (NIV). We go beyond what the law requires.

12. Martyn Lloyd-Jones, *Romans: An Exposition of Chapter Six* (Grand Rapids, MI: Zondervan, 1972), p. 268–269.

13. Charles Swindoll, *The Tale of the Tardy Oxcart* (Nashville, TN: Word, 1998), p. 304.

ETHICS

13

STRESS AND PRESSURE

The tiny country of Israel seems to be in the news most days. This nation that sits on the edge of the beautiful Mediterranean Sea has been the topic of conversation for thousands of years. It has withstood and persisted through incredible tragedies, overwhelming odds, and amazing difficulties. History reveals that it has fallen many times, but something within has given it a "psychological hardness" to withstand stress and pressure and become a serious leader in the world of military expertise.

The first king of Israel was a man named Saul. He was a tall, strong leader, and quickly took control as the nation's first administrator. Saul led Israel for over four decades. This king had security, was the right man for the job, and had the basic instincts to defeat virtually any aggressor. Originally, it was intended for him and his family to lead the nation for generations. However, in the midst of intense pressure, he made a decision that would change his future. He permitted the stress of the moment to get to him and he boldly took matters into his own hands and made a decision that was wrong. He not only ended up losing his status, but his rash choice eventually took his life.

He was faced with a unique dilemma. His military "special forces" became frightened, they wanted to run and hide because the panic of battle and the sight of the enemy had overwhelmed them. Instead of being a leader that takes control of the situation, he let the fear of the day get to him. He violated a basic rule of leadership. When adversity comes, leaders welcome it. In fact, they greet challenge as a friend.

We all have days, weeks, and months like this. What do we do when they come? Many leaders hold steady, don't submit to panic, and begin to clearly focus on doing the right thing. *Passion* to do the right thing is the attitude that separates those who make the right decision and those who choose to listen to the stress of the day and compromise. A leader must have determination to not listen to the panic of the moment but to find the quiet voice of counsel. In the midst of battle, the leader has to find enough "calm" to think clearly and react quickly. This passion to do what is right can cut through fear and pressure and help you make the next accurate decision.

While some leaders yield to the pressure and make wrong decisions, others have the same pressure and make right decisions.

> ❧ IT ISN'T STRESS THAT MAKES US FALL — IT'S HOW WE RESPOND TO STRESSFUL EVENTS.

Ensign Ross Rogers had been out of his training at Annapolis only a few weeks when he took his first duty station on the USS *Indianapolis*. He grew up in Paris, Tennessee. Solid Christian roots, a close family, and a good work ethic were at the core of this young officer. His decision to enter the navy as an officer came from his sense of loyalty to his nation and the necessity to become involved in a war that challenged our country's freedom, much like "9-11" has. The *Indianapolis* had only been out to sea on this trip for two weeks. Rogers and his shipmates left the port of San Francisco and quickly headed into the beautiful Pacific in July of 1945. July is a good time to cross the Pacific. The weather is normally favorable and the temperature is pleasant. Though the ship was carrying the bomb that would end the war, the crew knew nothing about this trip's significance. They routinely enjoyed the peacefulness that comes from the sea while the uncertainties of war were ever present on their minds.

When the challenge of their lifetime came — many were not ready. The enemy doesn't warn its target. Emergencies do not make appointments, and the greatest battles of life are often surprises. The nightmare began a few days after dropping off the top secret cargo on a small desolate piece of real estate called Tinian, that is ten miles long by three miles wide. On July 30, 1945, at just past midnight, a Japanese submarine saw the ship through the foggy haze. They had been waiting, and hoping for such an opportunity. At 12:05 the enemy silently, quickly took their aim and torpedoed the ship that housed approximately 1,200 men. With the impact of the direct hit, an estimated 300 men were killed almost instantly. About 900 men were in the warm but savage Pacific within minutes. Over the next 96 hours, the ocean, sharks, hypothermia, and dementia had taken the lives of all but 317 men.

> ❧ LEADERS ARE THOSE WHO MAKE THE MOST OF EVERY MOMENT, OF EVERY OPPORTUNITY, AND OF EVERY AVAILABLE RESOURCE.
> — THEODORE ROOSEVELT

In his early twenties, Ensign Rogers could never have dreamed that he would face such panic. The hit of the torpedo was not expected, and the ship was doomed from that moment. The events of his life unfolded without hesitation. Decisions were made instantly. Intense stress had kicked him into gear and his body's adrenaline and his refusal to submit to the panic saved his life and the lives of many sailors.

Rogers remembered being swamped by the water. He was possibly several stories up in the crow's nest when his jump plunged him deep into the blackness. He frantically found himself gulping diesel fuel, and swimming, hopefully, to the surface. Richard Newcomb writes in his book *Abandon Ship*, "Rogers was one of the last to leave the ship, and when he hit the water he went down, down, down. He thought he would never come up, but he did, and right in front of him was a raft. He grabbed a hand rope on the side and hung on as the ship reared above him, hesitated a moment, and then plunged. It was unbelievable that anything as big and safe and solid could disappear in a moment, but she did."[1]

Rogers climbed into the raft and met his three new shipmates. Gasping for air, trying to calculate what had happened, and assessing the situation were his instant responses. Over the next few days, he was credited with saving the lives of many men. He received the nickname of "Doc" because of his quick response to tourniquet a severe wound and cut the loss of blood of a sailor named Ferguson. He became the "commander" of four rafts and 19 men,

STRESS AND PRESSURE

including a couple of Marines. Dozens were crushed with the panic of the moment; however, "Doc" Rogers quickly moved into gear and, over the next hours, because of his level head, became a hero. This young ensign was my father-in-law.[2] My wife has the same steadiness as her dad, and she has greatly influenced my life during times of intense stress and unique pressures.

As long as you really believe what you're doing is right, you can cut through fear and exhaustion and take the next step.

Why some leaders panic under pressure and prolonged stress and why some make "heroic" decisions is something that has been called "psychological hardness." It's not stubbornness, meanness, or rudeness. It is a resolve to mentally hold steady, think clearly, and move quickly into the right choices.

There are three key assumptions these leaders quickly come to when faced with pressure and stress.

First, they feel *a strong sense of control*, believing that they can beneficially influence the direction and outcome of whatever is going on around them through their own efforts. Lapsing into powerlessness, and feeling like a passive victim of circumstances seem like a waste of time to them. Second, they're *strong in commitment*, believing that they can find something in whatever they're doing that's interesting, important, or worthwhile. They're unlikely to engage in denial or to feel disengaged, bored, and empty.

Third, they feel *strong in challenge*, believing that personal improvement and fulfillment come through the continual process of learning from both negative and positive experiences. They feel that it's not only unrealistic but also stultifying to simply expect, or even wish for, easy comfort and security.

Psychological hardness is a condition in which stress does not promote sickness or bad decisions but instead promotes success.[3]

As leaders, we understand that when times are stable, and the sea is calm and secure — no one is really tested.

When things are going along routinely and life seems peaceful, no one takes the opportunity to dig inside and discover the courage and deep "soul" character issues that are at the heart of who they are. In contrast, hardships, business crisis, and pressures force us to come face to face with who we really are and what we can become.

Paul wrote:

> I think you ought to know . . . about the trouble we went through.
> . . . We were crushed and completely overwhelmed, and we thought
> we would never live through it. . . . But as a result, we learned not to
> rely on ourselves but on God who can raise the dead (2 Cor. 1:8–9;
> NLT).

The "trouble" was a heavy-pressure situation. The ancient Greek word was used to depict a victim who was first tied up with a rope and laid on his back, then a huge, heavy boulder was slowly lowered upon him until he was crushed. Stress and pressure can put "the squeeze" on your emotions and rash decisions can be made without much thought — just to get relief. Paul is talking about mental suffering. Physical suffering is one thing, but emotional suffering can break both the body and the mind. Paul's greatest suffering was not physical, but mental. He goes on to say "we were crushed and completely overwhelmed." Again, the original language is talking about stress that is beyond anything that is normal or expected . . . something that is excessive and beyond the normal range of what most would experience. He thought he would not live through it. He felt there was no way out; he was trapped, caught, pinned down, emotionally pressured to a point of hopelessness. This biblical leader makes it very clear. His primary suffering at this moment of his life was mental, not physical. He is describing a pressure that few of us have experienced. What did this intense stress do to him? The answer is not so much what it did to him; it is what he did with it.

> ❧ ROUTINE AND PREDICTABLE DAYS ARE THE BREEDING GROUNDS FOR COMPLACENCY.

When you have exhausted your mental and emotional resources, you can no longer rely on yourself. You simply have to trust something; someone stronger, wiser, and smarter than yourself. "God who can raise the dead" was Paul's choice. What is yours? God delivered Paul — and God can deliver you.

He has rescued you in the past, He will rescue you now, and He will in the future. Stay where you are, hold steady, and trust. Don't listen to the temptation to act out of character or react badly to the emotional weight that you are experiencing. Great men fall when they break under the pressure. You do not need to break. You do not need to give up or give in to pressure. God can give you the "psychological hardness" to keep you in mental control.

Wally Armstrong and Jim Sheard teach golf clinics worldwide and have written three best-selling books on life, golf, and faith. They talk about maintaining balance in your golf swing and in life. One can only imagine the pressures of the course for the professional. However, when watching them it looks so smooth, routine, easy — though we all know that this game is a challenge. Armstrong and Sheard advise us to:

STRESS AND PRESSURE

- Build our life and our golf swing on a *solid foundation*.
- Build upon that foundation with *fundamentals that will withstand the challenges* of the course.
- *Apply those fundamentals on a daily basis* as we live life and play golf.[4]

BALANCE, FUNDAMENTALS, PSYCHOLOGICAL HARDNESS — ALL ARE CRITICAL

Quarterback Kurt Warner understands the fundamentals of life and football. He quickly rose to the top, taking the St. Louis Rams from worst-to-first. This MVP quarterback in Super Bowl XXXIV said, as he prepared to throw the bomb that won the game, "I began to pray." His autobiography, *All Things Possible* (Harper Collins, 2000) tells his incredible story "from rags to riches." He says, "Any power or peace I feel, on the football field or otherwise, is because of my faith and my relationship with Jesus."

The popularity and starting spot with the Rams didn't last. But his foundation in life did. The stress of the game, and the stress that comes with not being "on your game" didn't throw this man off track. Though he plays exceptional football, he and his wife, Brenda, have created a ministry called *First Things First*, an organization that reaches out to people in tough situations. Why do they do this? Because, not many years ago they were in a difficult pit where they saw no way out.

> ❧ EVERY GREAT
> LEADER HAS
> INCREDIBLE ODDS
> TO OVERCOME.

Brenda was a single mother with two children, living on food stamps. Kurt had no job, no money, no car — and no faith. Brenda wanted a husband, a companion, but would not compromise in her foundation of faith and marry anyone who was a non-believer. She talked to and prayed for Kurt for five years. He finally committed his life to Jesus Christ. *First Things First* is focused on the Bible verse, "But seek ye first the kingdom of God, and his righteousness; and all these things shall be added unto you" (Matt. 6:33; KJV).

Kurt and Brenda Warner have pressures, demands, and constant requests for their time and talent. Kurt says if anyone could say, "I'm too busy to pray," or "I'm too busy to read the Bible," it would be Kurt Warner.

"But I find if I spend time with God each day, He helps me sort out my other priorities," Kurt says. "Plus, whether I spend time in prayer or not, I'm still busy. So I may as well spend time in prayer and let Him help me! You have to give God time," he says. "I was trying to work God into my schedule. But God said, 'You need to work your schedule around Me.' "

ONLY ADVERSITY PRODUCES THE OPPORTUNITY FOR GREATNESS

Jesus taught his staff how to handle pressure. "Let's get away from the crowds for a while and rest." There were so many people coming and going that Jesus and his apostles didn't even have time to eat (Mark 6:31; NLT).

Even for Jesus, life seemed to be out of control. The pressures and stress that He experienced were far more significant than any we will face. Yet, He didn't make bad decisions, react impulsively, or go into verbiage that was out of control. He held steady, remained calm, and maintained His balance. What can we learn?

He knew himself. "I am the light of the world" (John 8:12; NLT). On at least 18 occasions, Jesus informed people who He was. Privately, He understood His gifts, purpose, and what He was to do. If you are not certain of who you are, you will let others fit you into their mold. You will also permit the stress of the day to get to you and prompt you to make unwise decisions.

He knew His boss. "But I do nothing without consulting the Father" (John 5:30; NLT). Jesus understood the rules, who He was serving, and what He needed to do. While He listened to His followers, He didn't permit other voices, people's opinions, and the "whiners" to push Him into their wishes. He didn't fear rejection. He made clear decisions knowing that He wouldn't please everyone. Leaders understand the uncompromising rules and they know the right "boss."

He was goal oriented. "I know where I came from and where I am going" (John 8:14; NLT). Leaders understand that if they don't set goals, someone else will persuade them to follow their goals. Vision and goals will enable you to overcome the pressures of outside voices. When you procrastinate and don't determine where you are going, you will end up working for those you are asked to lead.

He was focused. ". . . they begged him not to leave them. 'I must preach the Good News of the Kingdom of God in other places, too, because that is why I was sent' " (Luke 4:42–43; NLT). Jesus knew how to listen with compassion, but He didn't let the other voices keep Him from His primary purpose. Leaders hear the concerns of the day, but they quickly prioritize and stay on course. They understand that they can only fight one battle at a time and they must pick their battles carefully.

Seventy percent of all U.S. workers say they feel moderate to great stress on the job. Most — 54 percent — cite the demands of the job itself for their stress. Only 10 percent blame their boss! (*USA Today*, Oct. 29, 2002).

He handed the "baton of leadership" off. "Then he selected twelve of them to be his regular companions" (Mark 3:14; NLT). No man is an island. If you try to lead and live life alone the tension is too much. The necessity of delegation is part of what great leaders understand. The larger your company, church, or organization becomes, the more you will need to equip, delegate, and empower people. Every leader makes decisions a little differently. The people you delegate responsibility to will not make decisions exactly like you. But when properly instructed and carefully managed, they will call the shots that are in the "good enough" category.

He prayed, took time to think, and found small moments of solitude. "Jesus awoke long before daybreak and went out alone into the wilderness to pray" (Mark 1:35; NLT). All leaders are busy. Time management is critical. Solitude is something we crave. But, everyone has 96 15-minute periods of time every day. All of us have seven days in each week. The president does, the CEO and CFO do, and Jesus did. He understood the importance of getting alone daily and praying. Leaders can talk to their creator about the pressures of the day and the stress they feel all around them. They can gain wisdom about how to organize and prioritize their day and read the Bible and understand accurate advice about how to live their life.

He enjoyed life. "Let's get away from the crowds for a while and rest" (Mark 6:31; NLT). A day off, a vacation, and some evenings free are all designed to give you energy and to help you think creatively. If you don't find ways to enjoy your life and "get away from the crowd for a while and rest," you will burn out. Bad decisions often come out of times of being too tired. Leaders can decide to do the wrong thing — just because they want relief from the pressure. The antidote? Plan rest and plan relaxation. Put your vacation, days away to think, and family times, on your schedule — before anyone else fills those times.

No question, stress and pressure can get to you. Every leader reacts to stress and anxiety differently, depending in part on his personality style, history, and the type of situation he is dealing with.

Your spiritual connection and growth is one of the best ways you can combat this challenge that is part of every leader's life. Attending religious services, joining a spiritual community, praying regularly, or having a deeper commitment to a spiritual life, have all been proven to calm the mind.[5]

Great men fall for good reasons. It's predictable most of the time. We started this chapter talking about the first king of Israel. Saul imploded under the pressure of stress, fear, and impatience. Ensign Rogers didn't. You know of great leaders that have made "stupid decisions" when they are under the gun. You don't have to make the same choices.

Endnotes

1. Richard F. Newcomb, *Abandon Ship! Death of the U.S.S. Indianapolis* (New York: Henry Holt and Company, 1958), p. 115.

2. Tragically, a drunk driver killed Ross Rogers when he was 44 years old.

3. James M. Kouzes and Barry Z. Posner, "Challenge Is the Opportunity for Greatness," *Leader to Leader*, Number 28 (Spring 2003): p. 19.

4. Wally Armstrong and Jim Sheard, "Balanced Swings," *Life@Work Journal*, volume 3, number 6, p. 82 (italics mine).

5. Karen S. Peterson, "Ways to Calm the Mind," *USA Today* (May 27, 2003): p. 6D.

MONEY

INTEGRITY INCLUDES OUR PHYSICAL SELF AND OUR FINANCIAL SELF

Elisha was the CEO of prophets. Elijah coached him. As Elisha assisted, watched, and listened to Elijah, he grew hungry to become like him — better than him. Not in an arrogant, egotistical way, but because Elijah's life worked and God was on his side.

Every leader wants to be successful. Success leaves clues — so does failure. Elisha wanted the same leadership stuff that Elijah had and wanted to get to a higher level. Elijah told Elisha the details of how God would take him from this earth, and that it wouldn't be long. The mentored became even more desperate to learn all he could from the mentor. Elisha's response was that he wanted twice as much supernatural power — "a double portion" — of what Elijah had. He couldn't keep his eye off his friend and elder prophet. At the moment of Elijah's departure, the leadership transition would be complete. Elisha needed to be present when the event happened. The Bible tells us, "As they were walking along and talking together, suddenly a chariot of fire and horses of fire appeared and separated the two of them, and Elijah went up to heaven in a whirlwind" (2 Kings 2:11; NIV).

Minutes later, other prophets saw Elisha's response and observed; "The spirit of Elijah is resting on Elisha" (2 Kings 2:15; NIV). The transition worked; the prophetic power was now in Elisha.

It often works that way. The servant becomes like the leader, the vice president becomes like the president, the administrative assistant becomes like the CEO, and "the apple doesn't fall far from the tree."

> ❧ THE SPIRIT OF
> AN ORGANIZATION
> IS CREATED FROM
> THE TOP.
>
> — PETER DRUCKER

Peter Drucker said, "If an organization is great in spirit, it is because the spirit of its top people is great. If it decays, it does so because the top rots; as the proverb has it, 'Trees die from the top.' No one should ever be appointed to a senior position unless top management is willing to have his or her character serve as the model for subordinates."[1]

Elisha also had an assistant. The difference was, Gehazi wasn't hungry to become entirely like his boss. He had a dark side — a secret agenda. Gehazi was like Judas, one of the 12 disciples (interns, if you will) of Jesus. Judas had a money problem. His temptation could have been the issue that not only took his "career," but also caused him to take his own life. Gehazi compromised his integrity in the way he chose to deal with money. Gehazi watched as Elisha refused payment for a miracle he performed on a military leader. Elisha didn't crave money or want reimbursement for something that he knew could be misinterpreted if he collected. As a leader, he trusted that he would always have enough and he understood from his mentor that great leaders are great givers. This commander wanted to pay Elisha: " 'Please accept now a gift from your servant.' The prophet answered, 'As surely as the Lord lives, whom I serve, I will not accept a thing' " (2 Kings 5:15–16; NIV).

Gehazi must have thought, *What are you doing? Take the money! You deserve it.*

Elisha didn't accept the gift because he wanted the commander to know that it was God who had healed him, not Elisha. It was a *money integrity* issue. Elisha had his financial convictions in order. The Bible tells us that Gehazi later went and found the commander and lied to him. He told the commander that Elisha had changed his mind and that he needed some of what had been previously offered. He said, "My master sent me to say, 'Two young men from the company of the prophets have just come to me from the hill country of Ephraim. Please give them a talent of silver and two sets of clothing' " (2 Kings 5:22; NIV). Gehazi wanted the payment that Elisha refused. He figured out a way to deceive the grateful military leader and take advantage of his heartfelt desire to pay for his healing. The commander gave Gehazi the money and stuff and Gehazi took it to his home and put it away. Elisha found out what his assistant did. Without hesitation, Elisha fired his assistant. The Bible tells us that Gehazi acquired the same illness that the commander was healed from. Elisha knew he could no longer trust him, and the mentoring of Gehazi was over. The assistant paid an incredible price for his lying, deception, and greed.

Gehazi's decision took his future. He could have had the heart of Elisha who desperately wanted to be like his mentor, perhaps even a double portion of Elisha's power and skill. However, he missed out when he chose to lie and covet the money that his leader refused. This reads like today's newspaper. The millionaire CEO who wants more, the religious organization that skips "common sense" and thinks they can double their money in 90 days. Innocent people get ripped off, because someone on top wants more. It's called "risk investment," but the bottom line motivation is the age-old attitude of covetousness — greed.

Gehazi had it; Judas had it; we hear of people who have it almost every day through the newspaper or news networks. The problem involves compromise with money. Something begins to enter their thinking and they compromise their ethical conduct with finances. Rationalization takes over and high risk becomes "not a big deal" investment. Pushing the books a little too far to build up a personal portfolio, or pulling budget from a designated area into your personal reimbursement or bonus package becomes the plan.

> Whoever trusts in his riches will fall, but the righteous will thrive like a green leaf (Prov. 11:28; NIV).

Like the problem with any moral compromise, if one is cheating on the dollars or cheating on their wife, they are likely cheating in other areas of life as well.

"In a quest for more ethical leaders, recruiters are increasingly looking into executives' personal lives for evidence of womanizing and other behavior that raises questions about their integrity. While there's no scientific proof that a philanderer is more or less likely to be involved in financial fraud, many executives implicated in recent corporate scandals exhibited other forms of questionable moral behavior along the way."[2]

MONEY

U.S. Attorney for Maryland, Thomas DiBiagio said, "If their life is a lie, it's not confined to their personal life. If they are lying to their wives, there's huge potential they are also lying to their colleagues, their board of directors, and potentially their auditors."[3]

The compromise with money, the giving in to greed, and the fixing of the books — whatever form it takes — is an integrity issue. Gifted leaders often let this hidden desire get to them. Some experts believe strongly that there is a connection between cheating on and off the job, which is one reason businesses often frown on extramarital affairs. "Fish rot from the head," says Robert Hogan, a psychologist and management consultant who is an expert in "dark side" traits. Hogan says it can be tough for people to make honest choices when they're leading double lives. "Some of my colleagues in psychology think there's a distinction between embezzling, compulsive lying, substance abuse, and philandering, but it's all a piece."[4]

> Whoever loves money never has money enough; whoever loves wealth is never satisfied with his income (Eccles. 5:10; NIV).

Throughout the years of working with religious organizations and churches, I have had to talk to boards and restructuring committees after a leader or pastor has compromised morally. Whether he had an affair, was hooked on pornography, or took money from the offering or general fund, I have learned to advise the board to look into other areas where he might have compromised. Check his credit card uses, his gas allowances, his perks, his computer, and other areas of his life. Often they find that he cheated in these areas as well, and that the problem was deeper than they had thought. If a man is willing to cheat in one area, he has probably opened his life up to other compromises as well.

We are often warned about how the elderly can easily be ripped off by liars, but it seems that Christians are often as naive to scams and swindlers. Whether it's too much trust in what people say (without doing our homework), or greed and our desire to want more — only the individual knows. Sadly, some innocent people have lost much of their retirement and savings because of greedy leaders.

Recently, Gregory Setser and the International Product Investment Corporation swindled churches and ministries under the guise of doing God's work. The case of the Securities and Exchange Commission has torn apart some of the largest ministries in the country, soiled otherwise unblemished reputations, cost investors an alleged $160 million, and has left many to question the investment advice of trusted religious figures.[5] Setser convinced popular religious leaders, evangelists, and pastors to invest money in a product with a 25–50 percent return on investment in 60–90 days. People like Ralph Wilkerson, the founder of Melody Christian Center in Anaheim, California, became involved and as a result influenced others to invest.[6] Many forgot the proverb "There are no free lunches in life."

While Setser was bilking hundreds of faithful Christians across the United States, Canada, and Europe, he was not living the humble lifestyle he often claimed. Setser created accounts in Hong Kong, Bern, Panama, Switzerland, Germany, and numerous other accounts in California, according to the SEC filings. At the time of his arrest, Setser and his organization owned a $2.3 million, 103-foot powerboat (that was kept fully staffed and at the ready off the coast of Mexico), a $1.1 million helicopter, numerous houses and real estate holdings, and several vehicles. He robbed Peter to pay Paul. He promised great returns and duped "famous" people into giving their company's money in order to feed his accounts and to cover up his deception. The list of people who bought into the scam includes not only Christian leaders, but also denominational officials. One denomination "invested" $14 million, another church group invested $2.3 million.

If anyone had done an in-depth search of Setser's history they would have found that he had learned some bad money habits. He pled no contest to "theft by check" in Texas in 1993, according to records. Shortly thereafter, he filed for Chapter 13 bankruptcy. Four years later, the court dismissed his Chapter 3 petition after he failed to make payments as agreed, according the SEC. Unfortunately, none of these facts was ever made known to his investors at the time he was duping new-found "friends" and "business partners."

Rejoice Ministries, a tiny church in Willmar, Minnesota, lost its pastor. He just disappeared — with $3,344 of the church's money. "James Poole" had recently accepted the job, and then asked for a salary advance to help with rent, a down payment on a new bathtub, and other expenses. He got the money, preached one Sunday, and then skipped town.[7] One wonders what his real motives were for assuming the pastorate of that church. Did he do it to rip them off? Or did he become the pastor and then decide to take the money and run?

> ❧ ONE UNCONTROLLED CHARACTER FLAW CAN RUIN YOUR GREATEST ACCOMPLISHMENT.

The love of money is a root of all kinds of evil. Some people, eager for money, have wandered from the faith and pierced themselves with many griefs (1 Tim. 6:10; NIV).

MONEY

This is another front-page story of greed, financial compromise, and deception. Sad to say, this temptation is among the easiest to which leaders can fall.

Our integrity most certainly involves our finances. God isn't against money, in fact some of the greatest leaders in the Bible have been wealthy. It's the greed, the craving for more, and fudging on our integrity to get more that greatly concerns God. Where is the balance? How does integrity with our finances work? Understanding the temptations is key.

Financial integrity is a lifelong journey. I don't believe a person can ever relax on issues of integrity. There are temptations around every corner — money deals, high-risk options, and even attractive scams. Smart people make dumb decisions all the time. The urge to want more no matter how much you have is something that is common among humans in general.

KNOW YOURSELF

With Noah, it was alcohol; Lot had a greed issue; Jacob used deception; Moses struggled with anger; Sampson, King David, and David's son Solomon dealt with a lust problem. For a time, Peter let fear control his behavior; both Judas and Gehazi could not control their craving for money. The Bible never tries to hide the temptations leaders have faced or the times they made out-of-balance decisions. That is one of the most encouraging things about the Bible. We can relate to people who have fallen, but also can see the grace of God and the way He restored their lives. Many learned from their failures and became better people. What are your weak areas? Alcohol, drugs, lust, greed, anger, fear, or a host of others are common weaknesses. What are yours? Knowing that answer is 50 percent of the battle. Once you know what you're facing, you can work on discovering what to do about it, where to get help, and how to get over it — with God's help.

> ❧ ONE OF THE GREATEST TEMPTATIONS LEADERS FACE IS INCONGRUITY.

KNOW YOUR TRIGGERS

"Bad behavior follows bad thinking like stink follows a skunk," writes Bill Perkins, author of *When Good Men Are Tempted*.[8] We first think about something we want, then desire it, and then find a way to get it — even if that means bending the rules a little — or a lot.

"For someone with an eating compulsion, the trigger may be buying the ingredients for brownies to make a treat for the kids. For the sex addict, it could be surfing the Internet or calling a former boyfriend or girlfriend 'just to talk.' For the alcoholic, it may be visiting a local pub for a soft drink."[9]

We have all heard it and perhaps done it. We know it's wrong, but we see it demonstrated so often. That is saying one thing and doing or being another. Incongruity is the cosmetic cover for hypocrisy. "Character is about aligning your lips with your life," says Mark Sanborn, author and professional speaker on leadership (www.marksanborn.com). Sanborn says that succumbing to temptation can be summed up with the question, "Why?" Leaders fail when "the focus is on 'what to do' and 'how to do it,' rather than 'why do it.' "

There is no perfect leader — all of us have weaknesses where we need to grow. "Ultimately, biblical leadership is about drilling deep until you hit bedrock, the ultimate way behind everything — life and physical death and everything in between — which includes leadership. And we've got to remember that leaders are held, biblically, to a higher standard. To whom much is given, much is expected. That suggests that the perks of leadership are matched by the responsibilities."[10]

"IT COULD NEVER HAPPEN TO ME"

In Steve Farrar's book *Finishing Strong* he points out some interesting research about pastors who failed as a result of an adulterous relationship, "Without exception, all of them believed 'it could never happen to me.' You are unquestionably the most vulnerable when you believe 'it could never happen to me,' " he said. "A leader's strength comes from his or her interdependency with colleagues, vendors, employees, friends, and family, and his or her dependence on God." In the real world — leaders fall.

Tom Mucco, a 30-year veteran of Procter and Gamble, believes that the unique temptations of a leader can be boiled down to four specific temptations — pride, ego, greed, and moral compromise. "I believe that pride is the biggest risk, but as an individual gets more responsibility, power, or influence, all four of these increase in their risk as temptations to be dealt with," Muccio said.

The resolve to resist temptation can be tiring, and if you have not taken the time to keep your life in balance, you can become weary in the fight. Muccio said, "Individuals may have started out very disciplined and constantly checking themselves for wrong motives or wrong actions. But the more hectic your pace, the more responsibility that you have, the more privilege that you're given, and the more deference that those who work for you are willing to give

MONEY

you, the easier it is to compromise. As your position of power increases, the ability to compromise or cut a corner here and there is very easy to justify. As the Word says, 'it's the little foxes that ruin the vineyards,' and I've found that to be true in this area as well."[11]

A gift opens the way for the giver (Prov. 18:16; NIV).

THE COUNTERBALANCE THAT WORKS

We have all heard the analogy; there are two kinds of people in this world — givers and takers. I think this is true. A Creator that by His very nature is giving, has created every person. "God so loved the world that He gave" (John 3:16; NIV). "The Son of Man did not come to be served, but to serve" (Mark 10:45; NIV). To resist the urge to give or serve goes against our nature. To find ways to be content with what we have while maintaining excellence in our gifts is to be like our Creator. To develop a plan to be more philanthropical is very much like the heart of God. "For God loves a cheerful giver" (2 Cor. 9:7; NIV).

A giving attitude literally fights the temptation to be greedy. The fear of not having enough is perhaps the leading reason for a breech of financial integrity. The remedy for this fear is in our understanding of the way God supplies the needs for those who help the unfortunate. I'm happy to see that the *Chronicle of Philanthropy* found, in a recent poll of the 400 largest non-profit organizations in the United States, that donations to charities have increased 2.3 percent over the last year.

He who gives to the poor will lack nothing (Prov. 28:27; NIV).

Giving, sacrifice, and a serving attitude will beat the temptation for greed. It will also demonstrate to your team that you are a giver, not a taker. This, in turn, will motivate them to have the same attitude. How much is enough? How much do you need? Many say, just another thousand, million, house, boat, or whatever. I want to propose that your focus be on how to give — not how to get.

John Maxwell said:

If a team doesn't reach its potential, ability is seldom the issue. It's rarely a matter of resources. It's almost always a payment issue. The team fails to reach its potential when it fails to pay the price. If you lead a team, then one of the difficult things you must do is convince your teammates to sacrifice for the good of the group. The more talented the team members, the more difficult it may be to convince them to put the team first.

Begin by modeling sacrifice. Show the team that you are willing to:

- Make financial sacrifices for the team.
- Keep growing for the sake of the team.
- Empower others for the sake of the team.
- Make difficult decisions for the sake of the team.

Once you have modeled a willingness to pay your own price for the potential of the team, you have the credibility to ask others to do the same. Then when you recognize sacrifices that teammates must make for the team, show them why and how to do it. Then praise their sacrifices greatly to their teammates.[12]

Your integrity includes how you handle money. How you handle money comes from your nature. Givers get. Takers lose. Great leaders must demonstrate the attitude of a servant and the integrity that can be seen in their decisions, conversations, friendships, and checking account.

Endnotes

1. Peter Drucker, *The Daily Drucker* (New York, NY: Harper Business, 2004), p. 3.
2. Jayne O'Donnell and Greg Farrell, "Business Scandals Prompt Look into Personal Lives," *USA Today* (November 5, 2004): p. B1.
3. Ibid., p. B2.
4. Ibid.
5. *The Church Report* (September 2004): p. 18.
6. Ibid.
7. Ted Olsen, "Bilking the Brethren," *Christianity Today* (January 2005): p. 10.
8. *The Life Work Journal*, volume 3, number 5 (September/October 2000): p. 55, quoting Bill Perkins, *When Good Men Are Tempted* (Grand Rapids, MI: Zondervan, 1997).
9. Ibid., p. 55.
10. Ibid., p. 55.
11. Ibid., p 57.
12. John C. Maxwell, *Leadership Promises for Every Day* (Nashville, TN: Countryman, 2003), p. 281.

MONEY

15

DEPRESSION AND MOODS

I have the opportunity of attending an ACC basketball game a few times a year. We enjoy living in what is called the triad, where three of the top ten teams in the country house their universities. My office is a few hundred yards from Wake Forest University. Duke and Carolina are 90 minutes down the road. Consequently, during basketball season, I spend a few minutes a week reading, listening, and forming an opinion why one team is better than another. I'm certainly not the one to look to for advice on who is the best or who will make the final four. However, I have discovered this about teams. To be the best, you have to know how to win on the road.

To win on the road, you have to know how to control your emotions. The "rush" that comes from the affirming crowd when playing at home is amazing. A team at the bottom of the conference has been known to take down the top-rated leader when playing at home. The discouraging drain that comes from the crowd when playing on the road can take a talented team down in front of the nation. Their skill, line-up, or experience didn't change just how they felt. Emotions can be your friend, they can be your enemy, or they can just *be*. One thing is for sure — every great team has to play on the road and the players have to ignore negative emotions. Every leader must learn the lesson of fighting through his down times and of doing the right thing no matter how he feels.

All leaders have moods — it's just a matter of degree. Learning to control our emotions and moods while paying attention to discouragement and possible burnout and/or depression is important. Thinking that we are not susceptible to moods is a mistake.

Psychiatrists treat more cases of depression than any other emotional disturbance. Eight to ten percent of Americans suffer from major depression at some point in their lives. Many more persons have symptoms of depression but do not seek treatment.[2]

We get depressed for a lot of reasons. It could be a hereditary factor, a major adjustment, trauma, surgery, or a series of stressful events that bring on emotional downward spiral. Prolonged stress that doesn't go away can lead to discouragement and, eventually, deeper depression. Some suffer from a chemical imbalance and can have manic depression. Ex-Oakland Raider lineman Barret Robbins went AWOL two days before he was to play in Superbowl XXXVII. His invisible pain of mental illness wasn't being treated — because he thought he could beat it himself. Jimmi Hendrix suffered from this same mood disorder. Dick Cavett, Kitty Dukakis, and Ted Turner have publicly acknowledged that their fight with this battle will last a lifetime.

The pressure of doing what we do can add up for all of us. Most do not have a psychological disorder. We are able to deal with stress and adjustments before we feel deeply depressed, but too much pressure in too short a time can be overwhelming to almost anyone.

There is no question — you are the most vulnerable when you believe *"it could never happen to me."*

When we are emotionally weak, we can make decisions that are not sound. We can risk too much or decide something that's morally wrong. We have all seen leaders, pastors, deans of universities, and CEOs make a bad or illegal decision because they were fighting an emotional battle that would not go away.

Pastors, priests, or university presidents can make the decision to start looking at pornography because they are burned out and depressed. For most, this choice of behavior is not typical for them — not a character issue. It is a bad way to get their head out of the dark mood that they have been stuck in.

We can easily become overworked and live in the vicious cycle of the tyranny of the urgent, constantly dealing with an emergency, a crisis, a conflict, or the tension of making a profit. The CEO has the pressure of projected growth and it is always on his mind — his emotions are affected. Schedules get out of control, conflict can happen in his marriage, and life loses its joy. In the middle of all this he makes a decision that he regrets and it takes his future. Normally he would fight the temptation to "cook the books," or take more than he earned. He would be able to manage temptations with "so in so" or to turn his head when a pornography site popped up on his monitor. But his emotional strength to fight the wrong thought is not there. He wants a rest from the pressure and a way out of his depression. This time, he yields to the temptation, makes the call, and pays the price. Little things add up; the pressure gets to him; he makes the wrong decision.

Catch all the little foxes before they ruin the vineyard (Song of Sol. 2:15).

SOME CAUSES

Out of control schedules and lives

The Bible tells us about a powerful prophet named Elijah. Alone, he courageously confronted hundreds of the evil prophets of Baal. These prophets had intimidated the people of Israel under the direction of King Ahab and Jezebel, his wife. The Bible tells us that they were two of the most wicked leaders in the history of Israel. Elijah watched as these political leaders made decision after decision that brought harm to the people. He must have said to himself, *Enough is enough — these people have gone too far.*

He challenged the prophets of Baal's ability to pray and persuade their false gods to answer their prayers. He put his God up against their false gods — in front of the people.

Elijah said, "I am the only one of the Lord's prophets left, but Baal has four hundred and fifty prophets. Get two bulls for us. Let them choose one for themselves, and let them cut it into pieces and put it on the wood but not set fire to it. I will prepare the other bull and put it on the wood but not set fire to it. Then you call on the name of your god, and I will call on the name of the Lord. The god who answers by fire — he is God" (1 Kings 18:22–24; NIV).

DEPRESSION AND MOODS

The crowd of people around them liked the challenge and wanted to see what would happen. Whose prayer would be answered? Which prophet was right? The righteous one — or the 450 others.

The Bible tells us that the prophets of Baal did as Elijah challenged them to do. They prepared the bull, put it on the altar, and began praying to their gods "from morning till noon." For hours they cried out to their god, begged, did unusual things like cutting themselves — but nothing happened. They looked like fools.

Elijah watched them all morning and then made his move. He arranged the altar, took the other bull and prepared him for the sacrifice, and in an act of defiance to these false leaders, he poured buckets of water on the altar, soaked the wood and the water filled the trench around it. He then prayed, "O Lord . . . answer me, so these people will know that you, O Lord, are God, and that you are turning their hearts back again."

Then the fire of the Lord fell and burned up the sacrifice, the wood, the stones and the soil, and also licked up the water in the trench. It was an amazing day for this prophet and for the nation of Israel.

When all the people saw this, they fell prostrate on the ground and cried, "The Lord — he is God! The Lord — he is God!" (1 Kings 18:39; NIV).

The emotion of the crowd switched from the 450 to the one. They made an immediate decision to believe in the God of Elijah. Elijah then commanded the people to seize the prophets of Baal and have them executed. Elijah not only won the challenge, he eliminated these false leaders. When Ahab told his wife Jezebel everything that Elijah had done and how he had destroyed their network of false prophets, she became infuriated and decided to kill him. "Jezebel sent a messenger to Elijah to say, 'May the gods deal with me, be it ever so severely, if by this time tomorrow I do not make your life like that of one of them" (1 Kings 19:2; NIV).

After all the miracles that Elijah had seen, and watching God answer his prayers in impossible situations, he suddenly became intimidated and ran from this queen. The 450 didn't frighten him, but the one woman did. The Bible tells us "Elijah was afraid and ran for his life. . . . He came to a broom tree, sat down under it and prayed that he might die. 'I have had enough, Lord. . . . Take my life, I am no better than my ancestors.' "

What a shift in confidence — faith to fear — strength to weakness — running away not aggressively dealing with the problem. Why does the Bible record this story? It is an example of a very tired executive. He was a great leader who put in long hours and experienced one win after another, and then depression hit. He was exhausted, out of strength, and out of balance. Slowing down was not an option and he ran out of optimism, hope, and faith. As a result, this queen threatened him and he decided to run and hide and ask God to end his life.

God didn't answer the prayer of Elijah to end his life. He uniquely helped him, fed him, gave him some rest, and got him back on his feet to live another day.

> For everything there is a season, and a time for every matter under heaven (Eccles. 3:1; ESV).

If we don't control our schedule — our schedule will control us. If we don't find a way to live a balanced life — our lives will get out of balance. Everyone has the same amount of hours each day. One leader controls his schedule, one leader doesn't. One leader manages his energy, another lives on adrenaline. Winning builds the passion to win more. Success in our business, occupation, or church can give us the rush of wanting to get to another level — just for *the feeling* of one more achievement.

Life can get out of control quickly; we become tired and don't see it coming. Our discouragement and depression can cause us to say or do something that we would not have said or done if we had been emotionally strong, rested and in balance. When you're overstressed, the little things put you over the top.

> ❧ IF YOU DON'T CONTROL YOUR TIME — SOMEONE ELSE WILL. IF YOU DON'T PROTECT YOUR DREAM — YOU WILL FULFILL SOMEONE ELSE'S DREAM.

Not feeling fulfilled

Many hit the peak of their career, and look around and find it isn't what they thought it would be. Midlife crisis, disappointment in something you thought would bring deep satisfaction, or finding out that your dream wasn't all you thought it would be can make one feel empty and overly introspective. Buy a sports car, or a second home, get a girlfriend, wear lots of gold jewelry, or experiment with a behavior you haven't tried before — all are classic jokes . . . and facts about men in midlife crisis. What do you do? All of us hit halftime. What do great leaders do when they reach the top of their field and find it empty? Bob Buford looks at this time in life as a tremendous opportunity. In his book *Finishing Well: What People Who Really Live Do Differently*, he states, "Most people have a pretty good plan for 'Life I,' but few can see their way forward into 'Life II.' 'Life I' has a multitude of clear role models and consists of fairly simple steps. You grow up some-where, go to school somewhere, form your own family, and go to work some-where. Then you retire and _____."

And what?

That's the point, Buford says, you have to fill in that blank on your own. And this is where Life II begins. He writes about how to fill in that blank with meaning and purpose — not just with sea cruises, poker games, and golf.[3]

Many have chosen to do the wrong things to give them an emotional boost or because they are unfilled and bored. They make a choice that they would not have made ten years ago. They have an empty feeling inside that craves for satisfaction and they start doing dumb things.

Bill Perkins said in *Awakening the Leader Within*, that leaders need to control their inclinations. He writes that leaders should not "pet the Grem-lin." Temptations are like those "cute, furry creatures from the movie." They may seem innocent at first, but they turn into monsters that destroy life. A bored, stressed or lonely leader may turn to, say, an alcoholic drink or a porn website to create what Perkins calls a mood swing — a way of eliminating the nega-tive feelings that leaders often face. "Initially," writes Perkins, "these things may seem harm-less. But the law of diminishing returns tells us that it takes more and more of the substance and a riskier behavior to make the mood swing."[4]

> ❧ IS THIS ALL THERE IS TO LIFE? I FOUND LIFE IN JESUS.
>
> — TONY HALL, AMBASSADOR, UNITED STATES MISSION TO THE U.N. FOOD AND AGRICULTURE AGENCIES

Or we could be going through a phase of pain in the company or church. The constant crisis, the challenge that won't go away, and the drain of your energy has become silent pain. Your pain and weakness can become your enemies because there is a tempter who will take advantage of your weakness.

Professional counselor Craig Ellison writes, "How does Satan try to take advantage of our pain? Satan's one and only goal is to destroy us. He is a master military strategist. Satan and his forces study each of us thoroughly in order to determine our particular pain profile. Pain points are our points of psycho spiritual vulnerability. Our pain profile is the particular pattern of pain that we have developed from rejection, isolation, inadequacy, inequity/victimiza-tion, identity confusion, anxiety, worthlessness, and spiritual disconnection. Once he pieces together his military intelligence, Satan tries to stir our pain up through manipulation of circumstances, other people, etc. He then offers us a variety of ways to relieve our particular pain points."[5]

The relief he offers is always wrong. The compromise, the moment of pleasure, the greed for more always crosses the line. You simply cannot go there — no matter what your emotions tell you.

> And the tempter came and said to him . . . (Matt. 4:3; ESV).

When we are overly tired, discouraged, or bored with life we can lose our perspective. The very thing we once avoided becomes the thing we crave. Your perception is your reality. You begin thinking that a certain something will bring you happiness, and then you make the wrong decision. The writer of Psalm 73 said, "Surely God is good to Israel, to those who are pure in heart. But as *for me, my feet had almost slipped;* I had nearly lost my foothold. For I envied the arrogant when I saw the prosperity of the wicked" (Ps. 73:1–3; NIV, italics mine). *Then* Asaph changed his perspective and focus and, as a result, his depression went away. "When I tried to understand all this, it was oppressive to me till I entered the sanctuary of God; *then I understood their final destiny*" (Ps. 73:16–17, italics mine). He got alone with God, thought about what he was contemplating, and evaluated what had happened to people who did the wrong thing. As a result, he stopped envying people who had more perks in life.

Emotional dream stealers

Your aspirations, dreams, and visions are your God-given potential. When your head is clear, your heart is right, and your motives are pure, you will find a passion in life. It will be the thought you wake up with in the morning and the plan that naturally comes to you when you take time to get alone. It will be the energy that gives you strength for another day. However, there are emotions that can take your dream. You're in control. What you do with the "dream stealers" will make the difference between reaching your goal or falling short, winning or losing, giving up or pushing through the barrier.

THE SIX "D'S" THAT WILL TAKE YOUR DREAM — COMMON MENTAL CHALLENGES THAT WE FACE

Distractions will take your focus.

If you don't keep your eye on the goal, you will not reach the goal. Every person who drives will learn to focus down the road, not ten feet in front of the car. Distractions come to all of us every day. We handle the crisis and do

> ❧ IT'S A LIFESTYLE CHANGE TO MOVE FROM BURNOUT TO BALANCE, AND YOU HAVE TO COUNT THE COST. YOU'RE GOING TO HAVE TO SAY NO TO THINGS, AND THAT WILL COST YOU REAL MONEY.[6]

what we need to do, but we cannot let the issue take us from our focus. Many become emotionally bogged down in the distractions and lose their focus; as a result they never achieve their dream.

Divisiveness will take the unity.

When there is divisiveness on the team, backstabbing, mistrust, or extreme tension, there is an emotion that feels like anxiety, and agitation. We must deal with divisive issues (without injuring our team's ability to have differing opinions) or the emotional drain will sap our strength. The Bible tells us, "How good and pleasant it is when brothers live together in unity! . . . For there the LORD bestows his blessing" (Ps. 133:1–3; NIV). When we are paranoid about who we can trust and who we can't, it will take our energy from doing what is important. Deal with crisis and divisiveness sooner, rather than later.

Discouragement will take your strength.

Discouragement is one of Satan's favorite arrows. One of the top reasons why clergy leave the parish ministry and executives quit is discouragement. The leaders become tired. They burn the candle at both ends for too long. Frustration, perceived failure, or real failure overwhelms them. As a result, they become fearful about what "could" happen. Discouragement will sap your strength and take the fun from what you do

Discouragement is the deflator of courage. All leaders need to find a way to beat this emotion and dig for strength to fight the challenge of the day. Sometimes one of the most spiritual things you can do is rest or go on vacation or play with your kids, and take time to think and clear your head. "May the Lord your God be with you, as he was with Moses. . . . be strong and courageous" (Josh. 1:17–18; ESV).

Disillusionment will take your vision.

Losing our focus because we are disillusioned, foggy, or our perspective has become too complicated will stop us from achieving the dream. We can start out full of energy and potential, but over the long haul we change. The executive becomes pessimistic, the pastor settles for mediocrity, the denominational leader gives up on growth, and the university president lets the challenge of fund raising replace his vision for the future. This common emotion often is the result of doing too much at the same time. We must prioritize, meditate, pray, and find some solitude. When you block out time to think about what is going on, the disillusionment fades and the vision becomes sharp again.

Jesus often withdrew to lonely places and prayed (Luke 5:16; NIV).

Disappointment will take your faith.

Success is often followed by failure. Yesterday's victory doesn't win today's battle. People will disappoint you, let you down, or not come through on time. People will often forget yesterday's victory and fear today's challenge. When these things happen, we become disappointed with the people we need to have faith in. When we are hurt, we can become isolated, stop empowering other leaders around us, and draw into a shell. This will not help. "You are only hurting yourself with your anger" (Job 18:4).

Our disappointment with others turns into silent anger. We can't change the situation by being angry or reverse the past with anger. There is no such thing as being a leader without being disappointed by people. Leaders find a way to work through, work around, or work over the challenging situation. Their personal faith remains strong.

Depression will take your hope.

When we are depressed, our creativity, energy, and hope for the future is diminished. Everyone has a few hours or even days of depression. When it lasts longer than a couple weeks or if we begin thinking irrationally, we need to get help. If you are going through normal "life" depressive moments you can learn to pull back, think, and focus on the task at hand. Remember that depression is an emotion — just an emotion. It's okay to experience "blue moods" and keep doing what you do. If we get stuck in depression and stay there, we lose our hope for the company, the church, or the future. Beat the "dream stealer."

There is a strength that can get you through negative emotions. Learning how to fight through moods by focusing on what is eternal and true is the answer. The mentor Paul "coached" the young Timothy when he was discouraged and wanted to quit. "But you, man of God . . . pursue righteousness, godliness, faith, love, *endurance* and gentleness. Fight the good fight of faith" (1 Tim. 6:11–12, italics mine).

May the God who gives endurance and encouragement give you a spirit of unity among yourselves as you follow Christ Jesus (Rom. 15:5; NIV).

Endnotes

1. Lee J. Colan, *Minds & Hearts* (Dallas, TX: CornerStone Leadership Institute), p. 20.

2. Paul D. Meier, Frank B. Minirth, Frank B. Wichern, and Donald E. Ratcliff, *Introduction of Psychology and Counseling* (Grand Rapids, MI: Baker, 1991), p. 278.

3. *Leader to Leader*, number 35 (Winter 2005): p. 55.

4. Lucas Roebuck, "Tackling Temptation," *Life@Work*, volume 3, number 5 (September/October 2000): p 54.

5. Craig W. Ellison, "From Eden to the Couch," *Christian Counseling Today*, Sin and Psychopathology, volume 10, number 1 (2002): p. 33.

6. Carolyn McCulley, "Damage Repair," *Life@Work*, volume 3, number 6 (November/December 2000): p. 76.

16

THE ONE WHO CAN KEEP YOU FROM FALLING

The 2005 tsunami disaster looked like the Grand Canyon when the experts explored the bottom of the Indian Ocean. Thousands of years ago, the Grand Canyon was once a disaster, too. Experts tell us that the incredible force of rushing water pushed aside the earth, and today we have a beautiful scenic attraction that is visited by thousands of people every year.

The tsunami, which brought tragedy, can become something useful. It can warn us, teach us, and give us depth of character. Many do not learn from their mistakes or storms in life. However, the failure can be your friend that teaches and guides — or it can be a paralyzing enemy that takes your future.

Great leaders have learned from their mistakes. They know what they have done. They feel the temptation just to give up, but one day they decide not to listen to that voice of defeat. They have made a choice to fight the fear and go on for another day, into another future, stronger,

> ❦ ONE REASON
> GOD CREATED
> TIME WAS SO THAT
> THERE WOULD BE A
> PLACE TO BURY THE
> FAILURES OF THE
> PAST.
>
> — JAMES LONG[1]

as a better judge of their behavior because of their tragedy.

I understand that there is a principle that the United States Air Force calls the "power of motion." Young pilots are taught "speed is life" which comes with a corresponding action of pushing the jet's engine throttles forward to increase airspeed. It goes like this. When the pilots encounter an in-flight emergency that threatens the loss of the jet, they instinctively maximize their airspeed. With the maximum speed, the jet will handle better — not worse. The pilot's margin for error lessens when he "pushes the pedal to the metal." The same principle works when the enemy outnumbers a Special Forces soldier. When a U.S. Special Forces team is confronted with a lethal situation where the odds are against them, they push themselves into high gear. They automatically apply purposeful, coordinated motion, which puts the enemy on the defense, and creates a new opportunity for them to win or escape for another day. The enemy's *attack* is suddenly put on the *defense* because of the Special Forces' response to the emergency.

The best defense is a great offense. The way to work through your fear of failure, or the extreme discouragement that comes because you have failed, is to turn it around and look at it as a life lesson. We fight through our mistakes and failures by maximizing our forward motion. Like the pilot or Special Forces soldier, when fear hits we speed up the attack. When discouragement comes we don't stop, we dig deep and fight it through. The enemies we feel after we have failed are discouragement, depression, embarrassment, shame, and a loss of hope. However, these enemies can sharpen our senses and give us opportunities we would not have without them. The enemy can kill you, or it can warn and motivate you to fight it and beat it.

Failure can be the greatest storm of your life. The depth of pain is an emotional Grand Canyon. However, it can be turned into a beautiful wonder that God will use to help you and those around you.

Why do we take that step that we know is too far? As I've explained, there are lots of reasons, rationalizations, and motives. I've listed only 14 of the most common ones, but there are many more. Watching what has happened to very talented, smart men should give us enough warning. However, something inside us drives us and says, "You can do this and get away with it — you're different."

But we're not. We all have feet of clay to some extent. Everyone has been tempted to do the wrong thing, all of us have made mistakes, and some of us are in the middle of a "high risk mistake" right now.

YOU CAN CHOOSE TO DO THE RIGHT THING

I believe that one of the greatest gifts God has given us is the freedom to make decisions — a life full of choices. We can choose to walk away from wrong opportunities; to evaluate, to think, and to decide not to participate. All of us who have fallen made a decision. All of us who have not fallen faced similar temptations, but made a different decision. We really can't blame anyone else. We made the call. And, all of us have made the "bad call" in some areas of our lives.

You can choose to let the One who created you help you with all that you do. The Bible tells us that Jesus Christ created you. *"He is the image of the invisible God . . . for by him all things were created"* (Col. 1:15–16; NIV). You can understand that He will help you with all of your decisions. When you connect with Jesus Christ by way of a personal relationship, He will walk you through everything you do. When you didn't know Him, you were only influenced by your own decision-making process or by the pressure that came from your peers; after you come to Him, you will be different. His influence on your life will guide you through your decisions in business, in your church, in your family, and with the friends you choose to make part of your life. We all fight similar battles, just camouflaged differently. If we rely on the strength that comes from Jesus Christ, He will not allow the enemy of our souls to give us more than we can take. The Bible tells us, "No temptation has seized you except what is common to man. And God is faithful, he will not let you be temped beyond what you can bear. But when you are tempted, he will also provide a way out so that you can stand up under it" (1 Cor. 10:13; NIV).

✢ IN THE STRUGGLE BETWEEN THE STONE AND THE WATER — IN TIME, THE WATER WINS.

— CHINESE PROVERB

THE ONE WHO CAN KEEP YOU FROM FALLING

> ❧ TOO MANY
> PEOPLE, WHEN
> THEY MAKE A
> MISTAKE, JUST
> KEEP STUBBORNLY
> PLOWING AHEAD
> AND END UP
> REPEATING THE
> SAME MISTAKE. I
> BELIEVE IN THE
> MOTTO "TRY AND
> TRY AGAIN." BUT
> THE WAY I READ IT,
> IT SAYS, "TRY, THEN
> STOP AND THINK.
> THEN TRY AGAIN."
> — WILLIAM DEAN
> SINGLETON[3]

Billy Graham, Rick Warren, Pope John, and Mother Teresa — everyone — has been tempted. I have been tempted, you have been tempted, and we will continue to be challenged with issues that violate our conscience, our sense of ethics, or push us to sin against God. Why? "There is no one righteous, not even one" (Rom. 3:10; NIV).

We all face the temptation to do the wrong thing, but there is a way out. One day at a time, and at times one hour at a time, you can receive the courage, strength, and conviction to hold your ground. You do not have to make the choice to do what is wrong. When you give your life to Jesus Christ and make him your boss, CEO, director in all you do — your Lord — you will become connected to the One who made you. You are "wired" in a very unique way by the Creator of everything. There never has been and there never will be another person quite like you. When you know your Creator, you will begin to understand and fulfill the destiny God has for you. The Bible also tells us that every human being has a hunger to know the one who made him or her. Everyone has a desire to experience God. "He has also set eternity in the hearts of men" (Eccles. 3:11; NIV). Until you experience Him, there will be dissatisfaction in your life, a sense of hunger to know what life is all about, and a desire to know what happens after life is over. You can be forgiven and start again.

When we make bad decisions — wrong choices — we feel the impact. Many give up and divorce, run away, become bitter, or quit on life. I know of executives, pastors, priests, university leaders, and coaches who have stopped their pursuit of their life goals and basically quit trying — or worse. As the pastor of the Crystal Cathedral, Robert Schuler often says, "Turn your scars into stars." Don't let your bad experiences wipe you out.

All of us have made decisions we regret and all of us can be forgiven and start over. Perhaps it won't be in the same area of life or career track. It might not be with the same people or church. The consequences of our behavior might have cost us our job, ministry, or even the people we love. However, it didn't change the fact that God loves us — and wants to get us back on our feet. Our Creator will forgive us, and He will show us what to do next. "If we confess our sins, he is faithful and just and will forgive us our sins and purify us from all unrighteousness" (1 John 1:9; NIV). He can forgive us of anything.

What about those who are Christians and have chosen to do the wrong thing? The world (including the church world) we live in sometimes judges people of faith more harshly. The embarrassment, shame, and guilt can be overwhelming; however, the Scriptures tell us that Christians can make bad mistakes, too. The difference is that they already have a relationship with God and should understand that they can immediately go to God about their behavior. He will help us get back on our feet, forgive us, and help us not make the same decision again. "Dear children, I write this to you so that you will not sin. But if anybody does sin, we have one who speaks to the Father in our defense — Jesus Christ, the Righteous One. He is the atoning sacrifice for our sins" (1 John 2:1–2; NIV).

When you have a relationship with Jesus Christ, you change and become a man who is directed by your Heavenly Father — not by the influence from others. "Yet to all who received him, to those who believed in his name, he gave the right to become children of God — children born not of a natural descent, nor of a human decision or a husband's will, but born of God" (John 1:12–13; NIV).

> **FAILURE ISN'T TOO BAD IF IT DOESN'T GO TO YOUR HEART. SUCCESS IS ALL RIGHT IF IT DOESN'T GO TO YOUR HEAD.**
> — GRANTLAND RICE[4]

YOU CAN TURN YOUR FAILURE INTO YOUR FRIEND

Your greatest area of leadership often comes out of your greatest area of pain and weakness. The thing is — great leaders don't quit. Your weakness and failure can be your greatest friend. Paul Martin said there is nothing more important than persistence in success. He ought to know. In 1999, he finished 153rd, in the horrendous Hawaiian Iron Man triathlon, finishing ahead of 1,200 other athletes who had a significant advantage over him. They had both legs. Martin is an amputee who competed with a prosthetic leg. What is your attitude?

THE ONE WHO CAN KEEP YOU FROM FALLING

John Maxwell writes about the "thinking difference" between failing backward and failing forward.

Failing Backward	Failing Forward
Blaming others	Taking responsibility
Repeating the same mistakes	Learning from each mistake
Expecting never to fail again	Knowing failure is a part of the process
Expecting to continually fail	Knowing failure is a part of progress
Accepting tradition blindly	Challenging outdated assumptions
Being limited by past mistakes	Taking new risks
Thinking I am a failure	Believing something didn't work
Quitting	Persevering[5]

The Bible tells us that the one who created you will protect you. "If the LORD delights in a man's way, he makes his steps firm; though he stumble, he will not fall, for the LORD upholds him with his hand" (Ps. 37:23–24; NIV). We all stumble, trip, and occasionally fall. But "the Lord . . . makes his steps firm . . . the Lord upholds him with his hand." God wants to be very involved in your life and walk you through whatever life brings.

The LORD upholds all those who fall and lifts up all who are bowed down (Ps. 145:14; NIV).

When He becomes the CEO, the boss of your life, your Lord, everything becomes different. You think differently, dream differently, have a sensitivity that you never had, and have the privilege of letting the Creator assist you in all you do. You have been forgiven, and you are now connected to the one who thought of you before you were born. When He has forgiven you, He will give you a new perspective, and a new shot at life. The Bible says, "Once you were alienated from God and were enemies in your minds because of your evil behavior. But now he has reconciled you by Christ's physical body through death to present you holy in his sight, without blemish and free from accusation" (Col. 1:21–22; NIV).

You can talk to God right now and ask Jesus Christ to become the Lord of your life. It's really quite simple. No payback, no works you have to do, and no begging God for for-

> ❧ GREAT MEN DO NOT HAVE TO FALL. GREAT MEN CHOOSE TO WALK ANOTHER WAY.

giveness. God just needs your heart. "If you confess with your mouth, 'Jesus is Lord,' and believe in your heart that God raised him from the dead, you will be saved" (Rom. 10:9; NIV). Why not let the Creator help you? You don't have to make the same mistakes and you don't have to be afraid of life.

Endnotes

1. John Maxwell, *Failing Forward* (Nashville, TN: Thomas Nelson Publishers, 2000), p. 73.

2. Ibid., p. 35

3. Ibid., p. 51

4. Ibid., p. 23

5. Ibid., p. 8.

THE ONE WHO CAN KEEP YOU FROM FALLING

For over 20 years **Dr. Wayde I. Goodall** has been encouraging and ministering to individuals, community leaders, and over 32,000 fellow pastors on issues impacting families, marriage, and parenting.

He holds a Master of Arts degree in counseling from Central Michigan University and a Bachelor of Arts degree in Bible and one in psychology from Southern California College. He also earned Doctor of Ministry degrees from the Assemblies of God Theological Seminary and Northwest Graduate School of the Ministry.

He is a frequent speaker at conferences and conventions nationwide. As a former missionary and founder of Vienna Christian Center in Vienna, Austria, which today is one of the largest evangelical churches in Europe, he is often invited to be a speaker at international events and missionary conferences as well.

He has been active on a numerous boards and committees within the Assemblies of God, and continues to serve as adjunct seminary professor, as a guest teacher at the Billy Graham Cove in North Carolina, and as a frequent speaker on college campuses.

He recently received the 2005 Church Health Award from Purpose Driven, became a Certified Congregational Coach in 2005, and has been a worldwide host for the TCT television network. Wayde and his wife Rosalyn have two grown children, Jeremy and Kristin.